CHRONOLOGY AND DOCUMENTARY HANDBOOK OF THE STATE OF
SOUTH DAKOTA

ROBERT I. VEXLER

State Editor

WILLIAM F. SWINDLER

Series Editor

1979 OCEANA PUBLICATIONS, INC./ Dobbs Ferry, New York

HOUSTON PUBLIC LIBRARY

R01 0846 7832

Library of Congress Catalog Card No. 78-26887
ISBN 0-379-16166-4

© Copyright 1979 by Oceana Publications, Inc.

All rights reserved. No part of this publication may be reproduced or transmitted in any form or by any means, electronic or mechanical, including photocopy, recording, xerography, or any information storage and retrieval system, without permission in writing from the publisher.

Manufactured in the United States of America

Seal of the State of South Dakota

TABLE OF CONTENTS

INTRODUCTION	ix
CHRONOLOGY (1743-1977)	1
BIOGRAPHICAL DIRECTORY	20
PROMINENT PERSONALITIES	31
FIRST STATE CONSTITUTION	35
SELECTED DOCUMENTS	91
Facts About North Dakota - 1890's	93
The Black Hills District - 1890's	111
Among the Black Hills - Early 20th Century	133
Basic Facts	143
Map of Congressional Districts	144
SELECTED BIBLIOGRAPHY	145
NAME INDEX	147

ACKNOWLEDGMENT

Special recognition should be accorded Melvin Hecker, whose research has made a valuable contribution to this volume.

Thanks to my wife, Francine, in appreciation of her help in the preparation of this work.

Thanks also to my children, David and Melissa, without whose patience and understanding I would have been unable to devote the considerable time necessary for completing the state chronology series.

I also wish to acknowledge the scholarly research grant given to me by Pace University. This greatly eased the technical preparation of this work.

Robert I. Vexler
Pace University

INTRODUCTION

This projected series of *Chronologies and Documentary Handbooks of the States* will ultimately comprise fifty separate volumes—one for each of the states of the Union. Each volume is intended to provide a concise ready reference to basic data on the state, and to serve as a starting point for more extended study as the individual user may require. Hopefully, it will be a guidebook for a better informed citizenry - students, civic and service organizations, professional and business personnel, and others.

The editorial plan for the *Handbook* series falls into six divisions: (1) a chronology of selected events in the history of the state; (2) a short biographical directory of the principal public officials, e.g., governors, Senators and Representatives; (3) a short biographical directory of prominent personalities of the state (for most states); (4) the first state constitution; (5) the text of some representative documents illustrating main currents in the political, economic, social or cultural history of the state; and (6) a selected bibliography for those seeking further or more detailed information. Most of the data found in the present volume, in fact, have been taken from one or another of these references.

The current constitutions of all fifty states, as well as the federal Constitution, are regularly kept up to date in the definitive collection maintained by the Legislative Drafting Research of Columbia University and published by the publisher of the present series of *Handbooks*. These texts are available in most major libraries under the title, *Constitutions of the United States: National and State,* in two volumes, with a companion volume, the *Index Digest of State Constitutions*.

Finally, the complete collection of documents illustrative of the constitutional development of each state, from colonial or territorial status up to the current constitution as found in the Columbia University collection, is being prepared for publication in a multi-volume series by the present series editor. Whereas the present series of *Handbooks* is intended for a wide range of interested citizens, the series of annotated constitutional materials in the volumes of *Sources and Documents of U.S. Constitutions* is primarily for the specialist in government, history or law. This is not to suggest that the general citizenry may not profit equally from referring to these materials; rather it points up the separate purpose of the *Handbooks*, which is to guide the user of these and other sources of authoritative information with which he may systematically enrich his knowledge of this state and its place in the American Union.

William J. Swindler
John Marshall Professor of Law
College of William and Mary
Series Editor

Robert I. Vexler
Associate Professor of History
Pace University
Series Associate Editor

Under God the People Rule
State Motto

CHRONOLOGY

1743	March 30. The region of South Dakota was claimed for France by Louis Joseph and Francois de la Vérendrye. They planted a lead plate at present-day Fort Pierre.
1803	The present-day state of South Dakota was a part of the district of Louisiana which had been ceded to the United States as part of the Louisiana Purchase. The region remained in this district until 1805.
1804	Meriwether Lewis and William Clark explored the area.
1805	The present state was made a part of the Territory of Louisiana, remaining so until 1812.
1809	Manuel Lisa formed the St. Louis Fur Company to trade in the Upper Missouri Valley.
1812	South Dakota became a part of Missouri Territory, and continued to be under this jurisdiction until 1820.
1813	Manuel Lisa and the Missouri Fur Company abandoned their three forts in North and South Dakota after the War of 1812 broke out.
1817	Fort Pierre was formed as a fur trading post.
1820	The state of Missouri was formed. South Dakota remained unorganized. That part of the region east of the Missouri River remained unorganized until 1834. The western portion was not organized until 1854.
1825	Henry Atkinson and Benjamin O'Fallon negotiated peace treaties with the Teton Sioux Indians.
1831	The American Fur Company sent the steamboat, the Yellowstone, up the Missouri River to Fort Pierre. This trip began steamboat service on the Upper Missouri.
1832	The Yellowstone travelled to the mouth of the Yellowstone River.

SOUTH DAKOTA

       Prince Maximilian of Neuwied explored the region.

1834   The eastern portion of the state became part of Michigan Territory.

1836   The eastern portion of South Dakota became part of Wisconsin Territory.

1838   The eastern section of South Dakota became part of Iowa Territory.

       John C. Frémont explored the region.

1843   John J. Audobon and Edward Harris explored the area.

1849   The eastern portion of South Dakota became part of Minnesota Territory.

1854   The western section of South Dakota became part of Nebraska Territory.

1855   March 10. Marshall County, with its seat at Britton, was created. It was named for William Rainey Marshall, fifth governor of Minnesota, surveyor of Wisconsin Territory and member of the Wisconsin legislature.

       Fort Pierre was sold to the United States government. It was converted into a military post.

1856   A settlement was founded at Sioux Falls and then abandoned about six years later.

1858   Minnesota was admitted to the union. The eastern portion of South Dakota remained unorganized until March 2, 1861.

       The Yankton Sioux leaders ceded the southeastern part of Dakota to the United States.

1859   The <u>Dakota Democrat</u> was published as the first newspaper in the area at Sioux Falls. The paper was later called the <u>Northwestern Independent</u>.

1860   Augustana College was founded at Sioux Falls.

1861   March 2. Dakota Territory was established by a division of the Utah Territory. It also included portions of Wyoming and Montana as well as present-day North and South Dakota.

The Weekly Dakotan was first published. It is still published today as the Yankton Press and Dakotan.

1862

April 5. Bon Homme, Brookings, Devel, Lincoln, and Minnehaha Counties were established. Bon Homme has its seat at Tyndall.

Brookings, with its seat at Brookings, was named for Wilmot W. Brookings, member of the Dakota Council, speaker of the house, associate justice of the Dakota Supreme Court, and member of the state constitutional convention.

Devel, with Clear Lake as its seat, was named for Jacob S. Devel, member of the first and second Dakota territorial legislatures.

Lincoln County, with Canton as its seat, was organized December 30, 1867. It was named for Abraham Lincoln, United States Representative from Illinois and 16th President of the United States.

Minnehaha, with Sioux Falls as its seat, was organized January 4, 1868.

April 10. Clay, Union and Yankton Counties were created. Clay, with its seat at Vermillion, was organized January 3, 1863. It was named for Henry Clay, United States Senator from Kentucky and Secretary of State in the Cabinet of President John Quincy Adams.

Union, with Elk Point as its seat, was formerly called Cole County. Yankton, with its seat at Yankton, was named for the Yankton Indian Tribe.

May 8. Charles Mix and Hutchinson Counties were established. Charles Mix, with Lake Andes as its seat, was named for Charles E. Mix, United States Commissioner of Indian Affairs.

Hutchinson, with its seat at Olivet, was

named for John Hutchinson, acting governor and secretary of Dakota territory.

1863-65   Spotted Tail, Red Cloud and Sitting Bull led various Indian uprisings.

1870   Population: 11,776.

Part of the southern boundary of the Dakotas was settled.

1871   January 13. Hanson and Turner Counties were created. Hanson, with its seat at Alexandria, was named for Joseph R. Hanson, secretary of the first territorial legislature and member of the second legislature.

Turner County, with its seat at Parker, was established. It was named for John W. Turner, formerly a member of the Dakota territorial legislature.

1872   Part of the Chicago, Milwaukee and St. Paul Railroad was built from Sioux City to Yankton.

1873   January 3. The following counties were established: Armstrong, Campbell, Clark, Davison, Dewey, Douglas, Edmunds, Faulk, Grant, Gregory, Hamlin, Hand, Hughes, Hyde, Kingsbury, Lake, Lyman, McCook, McPherson, Miner, Moody, Spink, Stanley, Sully, Tripp and Walworth.

Armstrong, which later became part of Dewey County, was named for Moses Kendall Armstrong who had been a member of the Dakota territorial legislature and territorial council and United States Delegate to Congress from Dakota Territory.

Buffalo has its seat at Gann Valley.

Campbell, with its seat at Mound City, was named for Norman B. Campbell, a member of the Dakota territorial legislature. Clark, with Clark as its seat, was named for Newton Clark, a member of the Dakota territorial legislature.

Davison, with its county seat at Mitchell, was named for Henry C. Davison, an early settler. Dewey, with Timber Lake as its seat, was organized December 3, 1910. It was named for William Pitt Dewey, surveyor general of the Dakotas. Formerly called Rusk County, its name was changed on March 9, 1883.

Douglas, with its seat at Armour, was named for Stephen A. Douglas, United States Representative and Senator from Illinois. Edmunds, with Ipswich as its seat, was named for Newton Edmunds, member of the Dakota territorial legislature and founder of the Yankton *Press and Dakotan*.

Lake County has its seat at Madison. Lyman, with its seat at Kennebec, was named for W. P. Lyman, an early settler and member of the Dakota territorial legislature.

McCook, with Salem as its seat, was named for Edwin S. McCook, fifth secretary of the Dakota Territory. McPherson, with its seat at Leola, was named for James Birdseye McPherson, graduate of the United States Military Academy and brigadier general in the United States, who was killed at Atlanta, Georgia on July 22, 1864, during the Civil War.

Miner, with Howard as its seat, was named for Nelson Miner, a registrar of the Dakota land office, and Ephraim Miner, member of the territorial legislature and county recorder of deeds.

Moody County, with Flandreau as its seat, was named for Gideon Curtis Moody, member of the Indiana House of Representatives and Delegate from the Dakota Territory to the United States Congress.

Spink, with its seat at Redfield, was named for Solomon Lewis Spink, member of the Illinois House of Representatives, secretary of the Dakota Territory and Delegate from the Dakota Territory to the United States Congress.

Stanley, with Fort Pierre as its seat, was named for David Sloane Stanley, graduate of the United States Military Academy at West Point, commandant of Fort Scully and governor of the United States Soldiers' Home in Washington, D. C.

Sully, with its seat at Onida, was named for Alfred Sully, graduate of the United States Military Academy at West Point who fought in the Sioux, the Seminole, the Mexican and the Civil Wars.

Tripp, with Winner as its seat, was named for Bartlett Tripp, later president of the convention which drafted the South Dakota Constitution and justice of Dakota Territory.

Walworth,,with Selby as its seat, was named for Walworth County, Wisconsin.

Traffic began running on the Dakota Southern Railroad between Sioux City and Yankton.

1874 General George Armstrong Custer led an expedition into the Black Hills which discovered gold. In turn there was a rapid settlement of a large part of the western portion of the territory.

1875 January 11. The following counties were created: Custer, Lawrence, Pennington and Shannon.

Custer was named for General George Armstrong Custer, brigadier general in the United States Army who had explored the Dakota Territory.

Lawrence, with Deadwood as its seat, was named for John Lawrence, member of the Dakota Territorial legislature. Pennington, with Rapid City, as its seat, was named for John L. Pennington, fifth governor of Dakota Territory.

Shannon County, which remained unorganized and was attached to Fall River County for governmental purposes, was named for Peter C. Shannon, chief justice of the Supreme Court of Dakota Territory.

January 14. Brule and Potter Counties were established. Brule, with Chamberlain as its seat, was named for the Brule band of Sioux Indians.

Potter, with its seat at Gettysburg, was
named for Joel A. Potter, physician and
steward of the South Dakota State Hospital.

Gold prospectors began coming in to the
Black Hills Indian Reservation.

Spotted Tail, Red Cloud and Sitting Bull
led some uprisings which continued into
1876.

1876   Wild Bill Hickock was shot to death in
the Deadwood Saloon.

The Indians ceded their lands to the United
States in the Black Hills.

1877   Codington County was created, with Water-
town as its seat. It was organized on
August 7, 1878 and was named for G. S. S.
Codington, a Congregational clergyman and
member of the Dakota territorial legislature.

The Sioux Indians surrendered their claims
to the Black Hills. The gold rush reached
its height at this time. George Hearst
organized the Homestead Mining Company.

Settlers began the Great Dakota Boom for
farm land.

1879   February 22. The following counties were
created: Aurora, Beadle, Brown and Day.
Aurora, with Plankinton as its seat, was
named for Aurora, Roman goddess of the
dawn.

Beadle, with its seat at Huron, was named
for William Henry Harrison Beadle who fought
in the Civil War, was surveyor general of
the Dakota Territory, a member of the territorial house of representatives and later
president of the South Dakota House of Representatives.

Brown, with Aberdeen as its seat, was named
for Alfred Brown, who served as a member
of the South Dakota territorial legislature.
Day County, with its seat at Webster, was
named for Merritt H. Day, member of the
territorial legislature.

SOUTH DAKOTA

1880   Population: 98,268.

        The following academic institutions were
        founded: Dakota State College at Madison,
        South Dakota State University at Brookings
        and Yankton College at Yankton.

1882   The southern boundary of the Dakotas was
        set.

        South Dakota State University received its
        charter at Vermillion. It opened the same
        year.

1883   March 2. Butte County, with its seat at
        Belle Fourche, was created.

        March 6. Fall River County, with Hot
        Springs as its seat, was established.

        March 8. Roberts County was created, with
        its seat at Sisseton. It was named for
        S. G. Roberts, a book publisher and member
        of the South Dakota territorial legisla-
        ture.

        March 9. Jerauld, Sanborn, and Washabaugh
        Counties were established. Jerauld, with
        its seat at Wessington Springs, was named
        for H. A. Jerauld, member of the Dakota
        territorial legislature.

        Sanborn, with Woonsocket as its seat, was
        named for George W. Sanborn, superinten-
        dent of the Milwaukee Railroad division
        in South Dakota when the road was being
        constructed through the region in 1883.

        Washabaugh, which was unorganized and
        was attached to Jackson County for govern-
        mental purposes, was named for Frank J.
        Washabaugh, member of the territorial
        legislature and state senator.

        The following academic institutions were
        organized: Black Hills State College at
        Spearfish, Huron College at Huron, Sioux
        Falls College at Sioux Falls, and the Univer-
        sity of South Dakota at Sioux Falls.

1884   The state agricultural college was estab-
        lished at Brookings.

1885	November 3. The state constitution was ratified by the residents of South Dakota.

Dakota Wesleyan University at Mitchell and the South Dakota School of Mines and Technology were founded at Rapid City. |
| 1887 | February. The statute of the Dawes Allotment was passed.

March. An agreement was made with some Indians to open 11,000,000 acres, about one-half of the reservation, to settlement.

November. Residents voted their approval of the division of the Dakota Territory at the 46th parallel into two states: North and South Dakota. |
| 1889 | February 2. The United States Congress passed an omnibus bill authorizing the framing of constitutions for North and South Dakota, Montana and Washington.

February 7. Meade County, with Sturgis as its seat, was created. It was named for Fort Meade which in turn was named for George Gordon Meade. He fought in the Seminole, Mexican and Civil Wars. Meade was the victor for the Union at the Battle of Gettysburg.

February 22. President Benjamin Harrison signed the Enabling Act which paved the way for South Dakota's admission to the Union.

A state convention was called to meet at Sioux Falls.

July 4. The state convention readopted the constitution of 1885 with a few small verbal changes.

November 2. President Benjamin Harrison issued a proclamation which declared South Dakota the 40th state of the United States.

Arthur C. Mellette, Republican, became governor of South Dakota. He served in the office until January 1893.

Approximately 56,560 acres of lower Brulé |

lands were opened for settlement.

1890   Population: 348,600.

February 10. Approximately 11,000,000 acres of the Indian reserve were opened for settlement. The land lay between the White River and the Big Cheyenne and extending north from the Black Hills to the North Dakota boundary line between the 102nd and 103rd meridians.

December 15. Sitting Bull, chief of the Sioux Indians, was killed in a skirmish with soldiers.

December 29. Federal troops led by General Nelson A. Miles killed thirty Sioux Indians in the Wounded Knee Massacre. This symbolized the end of the Sioux resistance.

1892   Approximately 1,600,000 acres of Sisseton and Wahpeton lands were opened to settlement.

1893   January. Charles H. Sheldon, Republican, who had been elected in 1893, became governor of South Dakota. He served in the office until January 1, 1897.

1895   168,000 acres of Yankton Sioux lands were opened to settlers.

1897   January 1. Andrew F. Lee, Populist-Fusionist, who had been elected in 1896, became governor of South Dakota. He served in the office until January 8, 1901.

1900   Population: 401,570.

May 10. The Populist or Fusion Party held its national convention at Sioux Falls where it nominated William Jennings Bryan for President and Charles A. Towne for Vice President.

1901   January 8. Charles N. Herreid, Republican, who had been elected in 1900, became governor of the state. He served in the office until January 3, 1905.

Northern State College was founded at Aberdeen.

1903	Wind Cave National Park was created with 28,060 acres.
1904	416,000 acres of the Rosebud Reservation were opened to settlement.
1905	January 3. Samuel H. Elrod, Republican, who had been elected in 1904, became governor of South Dakota. He served in the post until January 8, 1907.
1907	January 8. Coe I. Crawford, Republican, who had been elected in 1906, became governor of the state. He served in the office until January 5, 1909.
1908	800,000 additional acres of the Rosebud Indian Reserve were opened to settlers.
1909	January 5. Robert S. Vessey, Republican, who had been elected in 1908, became governor of South Dakota. He served in the office until January 7, 1913.

February 26. Harding and Perkins Counties were established. Harding, with Buffalo as its seat, was named for J. A. Harding, speaker of the house of the 14th South Dakota territorial legislature.

Perkins, with its seat at Bison, was named for Henry E. Perkins, a member of the South Dakota Senate.

March 2. Carson County, with McIntosh as its seat, was created. It was named for Dighton Carson, a Wisconsin legislator, Nevada official and first judge of the supreme court of South Dakota.

March 9. Bennett and Mellette Counties were established. Bennett, with Martin as its seat, was named for John E. Bennett, a state supreme court judge, and Granville G. Bennett, Illinois legislator and associate judge of the Dakota Territory.

Mellette County, with White River as its seat, was named for Arthur C. Mellette, territorial governor of Dakota and first governor of the state of South Dakota.

1910	Population: 583,888.
1911	February 1. The state legislature ratified the 16th Amendment to the United States Constitution.
	Ziebach County, with its seat at Dupree, was created. It was named for Frank M. Ziebach, editor of the *Weekly Dakotan* and member of the South Dakota constitutional convention.
1913	January 7. Frank M. Byrne, Republican-Progressive, who had been elected in 1912, became governor of the state. He served in the office until January 2, 1917.
	February 19. The state legislature ratified the 17th Amendment to the United States Constitution.
1914	November. Haakon and Jackson Counties were established. Haakon, with its seat at Philip, was named for King Haakon VII of Norway.
	Jackson, with Kadoka as its seat, was named for John R. Jackson, member of the Dakota legislature and speaker of the house.
1915	The state legislature passed a law guaranteeing the safety of bank deposits.
1916	December 4. The state legislature ratified the 19th Amendment to the United States Constitution.
	Jones County, with Murdo as its seat, was created. It was organized on January 16, 1917 and was named for Jones County, Iowa.
1917	January 2. Peter Norbeck, Republican, who had been elected in 1916, became governor of the state. He served in the office until January 4, 1921.
1920	Population: 636,547.
1921	January 4. William H. McMaster, Republican, who had been elected in 1920, became governor of South Dakota. He served in the post until January 6, 1925.

CHRONOLOGY

1922	The South Dakota School of Mines and Technology opened the state's first radio station, WCAT.
1925	January 6. Carl Gunderson, Republican, who had been elected in 1924, became governor of the state. He served in the office until January 4, 1927.
1927	January 4. William J. Bulow, Democrat, who had been elected in 1926, became governor of South Dakota. He was reelected in 1928 and served in the post until January 6, 1931. Gutzon Borglum began work on Mount Rushmore National Memorial.
1930	Population: 692,849.
1931	January 6. Warren E. Green, Republican, who had been elected in 1930, became governor of the state. He served in the office until January 3, 1933.
1932	Various farm organizations worked to save South Dakota farmers from foreclosure.
1933	January 3. Thomas Berry, Democrat, who had been elected in 1932, became governor of the state. He was reelected in 1934 and served until January 5, 1937. January 20. The state legislature ratified the 20th Amendment to the United States Constitution.
1934	A new federal law, the Indian Reorganization Act, changed the government of the Indians and restored cultural activities among the Indian tribes.
1936	Mount Marty College was founded at Yankton.
1937	January 5. Leslie Jensen, Republican, who had been elected in 1936, became governor of South Dakota. He served in the office until January 3, 1939.
1939	January 3. Harlan J. Bushfield, Republican, who had been elected in 1938, became governor of the state. He was reelected

	in 1940 and served in the office until January 5, 1943.
1940	Population: 642,961.
1943	January 5. Merrell Q. Sharpe, Republican, who had been elected in 1942, became governor of the state. He was reelected in 1944 and served in the post until January 7, 1947.
1944	The United States Congress authorized the development of the Missouri River Basin Project, which included construction of Fort Randall, Oake, Gavins Point and Big Bend Dams in South Dakota.
1947	January 7. George T. Mickelson, Republican, who had been elected in 1946, became governor of South Dakota. He was reelected in 1948 and served in the office until January 2, 1951.
1949	January 21. The state legislature ratified the 22nd Amendment to the United States Constitution.
1950	Population: 652,740.
1951	January 2. Sigurd Anderson, Republican, who had been elected in 1950, became governor of the state. He was reelected in 1952 and served until January 4, 1955.
1953	The first television station in the state, KELO-TV, began broadcasting.
1954	March. Armstrong County merged with Dewey County.
1955	January 4. Joe J. Foss, Republican, who had been elected in 1954, became governor of South Dakota. He was reelected in 1956 and served in the office until January 6, 1959.
1959	January 6. Ralph E. Herseth, Democrat, who had been elected in 1958, became governor of the state. He remained in the post until January 3, 1961.
1960	Population: 680,514.

Ben Reifel became the first American Indian to represent the state in the United States Congress.

1961   January 3. Archie Gubbard, Republican, who had been elected in 1960, became governor of South Dakota. He was reelected in 1962 and served in the office until January 5, 1965.

February 14. The state legislature ratified the 23rd Amendment to the United States Constitution.

1962   Titan missiles became operational in the state.

1963   September 14. Quintuplets: four girls and one boy, were born to Mrs. Andrew Fischer in Aberdeen.

Construction of Oahe Dam on the Missouri River at Pierre was completed.

Minutemen missiles became operational in South Dakota.

1964   January 23. South Dakota ratified the 24th Amendment to the United States Constitution. It was the 38th state to ratify it. The Amendment was declared part of the Constitution on February 4.

1965   January 5. Nils A. Boe, Republican, who had been elected in 1964, became governor of the state. He served in the post until January 7, 1969.

February 19. Governor Nils A. Boe signed a bill which created new boundaries for the two Congressional districts of the state. It had been passed by the legislature on the same day.

1967   March 6. The state legislature ratified the 25th Amendment to the United States Constitution.

1969   January 7. Frank Fenner, Republican, who had been elected in 1968, became governor of South Dakota. He served in the office until January 5, 1971.

1970   Population: 665,507.

The United Sioux Tribes Development Corporation was established to help its members relocate and find jobs off the reservations.

1971   January 5. Richard F. Kneip, Democrat, who had been elected in 1970, became governor of the state. He was reelected in November 1974.

March 22. The "Railpax" routes were announced. South Dakota was not on the routes.

March 25. Congressional redistricting was enacted for the state.

1972   May 31. The Environmental Protection Agency approved the state's clean air plans.

June 9-10. A flood occurred at Rapid City, killing 242 persons.

George McGovern was nominated for the Presidency of the United States by the Democratic Party.

1973   February 2. The state legislature ratified the Equal Rights Amendment to the United States Constitution.

February 27-May 8. American Indian Movement (AIM) members occupied the village at Wounded Knee to protest federal Indian policies. The trading post was destroyed on April 29. There were two deaths and over 300 arrests.

1974   February 7. Richard Wilson, opponent of Russel Means and his American Indian Movement, was reelected president of the Ogala Sioux Indian Tribe.

August 16. Former United States Representative and Senator Karl Mundt died.

September 16. Charges of assault on government officers, conspiracy and larceny as a result of the 1973 occupation of Wounded Knee which were lodged against Dennis Banks and Russell Means were dismissed by a federal district judge.

CHRONOLOGY

November 5. Governor Richard F. Kneip, Democrat, was reelected.

1975   March 10. Russell Means, a leader of the American Indian Movement was charged with murder in commection with the shooting of Martin Montileaux of Leyle, South Dakota in a Scenic, South Dakota bar on March 1.

May 2. Highway patrolmen at Wagner in the eastern part of South Dakota had to use tear gas to remove eight armed Indians from the Yankton Sioux Industries pork plant.

May 9. State Attorney General Edward H. Levi announced the introduction of a new program designed to reduce crime in the state and improve the quality of criminal justice.

June 26. Two agents of the Federal Bureau of Investigation were shot and killed on the Pine Ridge Indian Reservation at Ogala approximately ten miles from Wounded Knee.

1976   May 5. Russell Means, leader of the American Indian Movement, was shot along with John Thomas, another member of AIM.

July 31. Democratic Vice Presidential nominee Walter F. Mondale visited Pierre and delivered the keynote address to the South Dakota State Democratic Convention.

August 29. President Gerald R. Ford met with Republican leaders in the area at Rapid City.

September 15. Democratic Presidential nominee Jimmy Carter visited a farm near Sioux Falls.

September 23. Republican Vice Presidential nominee, Senator Robert J. Dole, campaigned near Sioux Falls.

1977   April 4-8. A team of basketball players from the University of South Dakota and South Dakota State University visited Cuba where they played and lost two games to a taller and stronger Cuban national team.

BIOGRAPHICAL DIRECTORY

The selected list of governors, United States Senators and Members of the House of Representatives for South Dakota, 1863-1977, includes all persons listed in the Chronology for whom basic biographical data was readily available. Older biographical sources are frequently in conflict on certain individuals, and in such cases the source most commonly cited by later authorities was preferred.

ABOUREZK, James G.
    Democrat
    b. February 24, 1931
    U. S. Representative, 1971-

ANDERSON, Sigurd
    Republican
    b. Arendal, Norway, January 22, 1904
    Governor of South Dakota, 1951-55

BERRY, Ellis Yarnal
    Republican
    b. Larchwood, Iowa, October 6, 1902
    U. S. Representative, 1951-71

BERRY, Thomas
    Democrat
    b. ----
    d. October 30, 1951
    Governor of North Dakota, 1933-37

BOE, Nils Andreas
    Republican
    b. Baltic, S. D., September 10, 1913
    Governor of South Dakota, 1965-69
    Director, Office of Intergovernmental Re-
        lations, Executive Office of the Presi-
        dent, 1969-71
    Chief Judge, U. S. Customs Court, 1971-

BOTTUM, Joe H.
    Republican
    b. Faulketon, S. D., August 7, 1903
    U. S. Senator, 1962-63

BULOW, William John
    Democrat
    b. on a farm near Moscow, Ohio, January
        13, 1869
    d. Washington, D. C., February 26, 1960
    Governor of South Dakota, 1927-31
    U. S. Senator, 1931-43

BURKE, Charles Henry
    Republican
    b. on a farm near Batavia, N. Y., April
        1, 1861

d. Washington, D. C., April 7, 1944
U. S. Representative, 1899-1907, 1909-15

BUSHFIELD, Harlan John
    Republican
    b. Atlantic, Iowa, August 6, 1882
    d. Miller, S. D., September 27, 1948
    Governor of South Dakota, 1939-42
    U. S. Senator, 1943-48

BUSHFIELD, Vera Calahan
    Republican
    b. Miller, S. D., August 9, 1889
    U. S. Senator, 1948

BYRNE, Frank M.
    Republican
    b. Volney, Iowa, October 23, 1858
    d. December 25, 1927
    Governor of South Dakota, 1913-17

CASE, Francis Higbee
    Republican
    b. Everly, Iowa, December 9, 1896
    d. at the naval hospital, Bethesda, Md.,
        June 22, 1962
    U. S. Representative, 1937-51
    U. S. Senator, 1951-62

CHRISTOPHERSON, Charles Andrew
    Republican
    b. Amherst Township, Minn., July 23, 1871
    d. Sioux Falls, S. D., November 2, 1951
    U. S. Representative, 1919-33

CRAWFORD, Coe Isaac
    Republican
    b. near Volney, Iowa, January 14, 1858
    d. Yankton, S. D., April 25, 1944
    Governor of South Dakota, 1907-08
    U. S. Senator, 1909-15

DILLON, Charles Hall
    Republican
    b. near Jasper, Ind., December 18, 1853
    d. Vermillion, S. D., September 15, 1929
    U. S. Representative, 1913-19

ELROD, Samuel Harrison
    Republican
    b. near Coutesville, Ind., May 1, 1856
    d. July 13, 1935
    Governor of South Dakota, 1905-07

FARRAR, Frank Leroy
    Republican
    b. Britton, S. D., April 2, 1929
    Governor of South Dakota, 1969-71

FOSS, Joe
    Republican
    b. Sioux Falls, S. D., April 17, 1915
    Governor of South Dakota, 1955-59

GAMBLE, John Rankin
    Republican
    b. Alabama, N. Y., January 15, 1848
    d. Yankton, S. D., August 14, 1891
    U. S. Representative, 1891

GAMBLE, Robert Jackson
    Republican
    b. Genessee County, near Akron, N. Y.,
        February 7, 1851
    d. Sioux Falls, S. D., September 22, 1924
    U. S. Representative, 1895-97, 1899-1901
    U. S. Senator, 1901-13

GANDY, Harry Luther
    Democrat
    b. Churubusco, Ind., August 13, 1881
    d. Los Gatos, Calif., August 15, 1957
    U. S. Representative, 1915-21

GIFFORD, Oscar Sherman
    Republican
    b. Watertown, N. Y., October 20, 1842
    d. Canton, S. D., January 16, 1913
    U. S. Representative (Territorial Delegate
        from Dakota), 1885-89, (Representative),
        1889-91

GREEN, Warren Everett
    Republican
    b. Jackson County, Wis., March 10, 1870
    d. April 27, 1945
    Governor of South Dakota, 1931-33

GUBBARD, Archie M.
    Republican
    b. Huron, S. D., December 31, 1910
    Governor of South Dakota, 1961-65

GUNDERSON, Carl
    Republican
    b. Clay County, Dakota Territory, June 20,
        1864

d. February 26, 1933
Governor of South Dakota, 1925-27

GURNEY, Chan (John Chandler)
    Republican
    b. Yankton, S. D., May 21, 1896
    U. S. Senator, 1939-51

HALL, Philo
    Republican
    b. Wilton, Minn., December 31, 1865
    d. Brookings, S. D., October 7, 1938
    U. S. Representative, 1907-09

HERREID, Charles N.
    Republican
    b. Dane County, Wis., October 20, 1857
    d. July 6, 1928
    Governor of South Dakota, 1901-05

HERSETH, Ralph E.
    Democrat
    b. Houghton, S. D., July 2, 1909
    Governor of South Dakota, 1959-61

HILDEBRANT, Fred Herman
    Democrat
    b. West Bend, Wis., August 2, 1874
    d. Bradenton, Fla., January 26, 1956
    U. S. Representative, 1933-39

HITCHCOCK, Herbert Emery
    Democrat
    b. Maquoketa, Iowa, August 22, 1867
    d. Mitchell, S. D., February 17, 1958
    U. S. Senator, 1936-38

JAYNE, William
    ---- (Dakota)
    b. Springfield, Ill., October 8, 1826
    d. Springfield, Ill., March 20, 1916
    Governor (Territory of Dakota), 1861-63
    U. S. Representative (Territorial Delegate),
        1863-64

JENSEN, Leslie
    Republican
    b. Hot Springs, S. D., September 15, 1892
    d. December 14, 1964
    Governor of South Dakota, 1937-39

JOHNSON, Edwin Stockton
    Democrat

b. near Spencer, Ind., February 26, 1857
   d. Platte, S. D., July 19, 1933
   U. S. Senator, 1915-21

JOHNSON, Royal Cleaves
   Republican
   b. Cherokee, Iowa, October 3, 1882
   d. Washington, D. C., August 2, 1939
   U. S. Representative, 1915-33

JOLLEY, John Lawler
   Republican
   b. Montreal, Quebec, Canada, July 14,
      1840
   d. Vermilion, S. D., December 14, 1924
   U. S. Representative, 1891-93

KELLEY, John Edward
   Democrat/People's Party
   b. near Portage City, Wis., March 27,
      1853
   d. Minneapolis, Minn., August 5, 1941
   U. S. Representative, 1897-99

KIDDER, Jefferson Parish
   Republican (Dakota Territory)
   b. Braintree, Vt., June 4, 1815
   d. St. Paul, Minn., October 2, 1883
   U. S. Representative (Territorial Delegate),
      1875-79

KITTREDGE, Alfred Beard
   Republican
   b. Nelson, N. H., March 28, 1861
   d. Hot Springs, Ark., May 4, 1911
   U. S. Senator, 1901-09

KNEIP, Richard Francis
   Democrat
   b. Tyler, Minn., January 7, 1933
   Governor of South Dakota, 1971-

KYLE, James Henderson
   Independent
   b. near Xenia, Ohio, February 24, 1854
   d. Aberdeen, S. D., July 1, 1901
   U. S. Senator, 1891-1901

LEE, Andrew Ericson
   People's Party, Fusionist
   b. near Bergen, Norway, March 18, 1847
   d. March 19, 1934
   Governor of South Dakota, 1897-1901

LOVRE, Harold Orrin
    Republican
    b. Toronto, S. D., January 30, 1904
    U. S. Representative, 1949-57

LUCAS, William Vincent
    Republican
    b. near Delphi, Ind., July 3, 1835
    d. Santa Cruz, Calif., November 10, 1921
    U. S. Representative, 1893-95

MARTIN, Eben Wever
    Republican
    b. Maquoketa, Iowa, April 12, 1855
    d. Hot Springs, S. D., May 22, 1932
    U. S. Representative, 1901-07, 1908-15

MATHEWS, George Arthur
    Republican (Dakota Territory)
    b. Potsdam, N. Y., June 4, 1852
    d. Los Angeles, Calif., April 10, 1941
    U. S. Representative, 1889

MCGOVERN, George Stanley
    Democrat
    b. Avon, S. D., July 19, 1922
    U. S. Representative, 1957-61
    U. S. Senator, 1963-

MCMASTER, William Henry
    Republican
    b. Ticonic, Iowa, May 10, 1877
    d. Dixon, Ill., September 14, 1968
    Governor of South Dakota, 1921-24
    U. S. Senator, 1925-31

MELETTE, Arthur Calvin
    ----
    b. Henry County, Ind., June 23, 1842
    d. Pittsburgh, Kans., May 25, 1896
    Governor of Dakota Territory, 1888
    Governor of South Dakota, 1889-93

MICKELSON, George T.
    Republican
    b. Selby, S. D., July 23, 1903
    d. 1965
    Governor of South Dakota, 1947-51

MUNDT, Karl Earl
    Republican
    b. Humboldt, S. D., June 3, 1900

U. S. Representative, 1939-48
U. S. Senator, 1948-

NORBECK, Peter
    Republican
    b. near Vermillion, Dakota Territory (now
        South Dakota), August 27, 1870
    d. Redfield, S. D., December 20, 1936
    Governor of South Dakota, 1917-21
    U. S. Senator, 1921-36

PARKER, William Henry
    ----
    b. Keene, N. H., May 5, 1847
    d. Deadwood, S. D., June 26, 1908
    U. S. 1907-08

PETTIGREW, Richard Franklin
    Republican
    b. Ludlow, Vt., July 23, 1848
    d. Sioux Falls, S. D., October 5, 1926
    U. S. Representative (Territorial Delegate),
        1881-83
    U. S. Senator, 1889-1901

PICKLER, John Alfred
    Republican
    b. near Salem, Ind., January 24, 1844
    d. Faulkton, S. D., June 13, 1910
    U. S. Representative, 1889-97

PYLE, Gladys
    Republican
    b. Huron, S. D., October 4, 1890
    U. S. Senator, 1938-39

SHARPE, Merrell Quentin
    Republican
    b. Marysville, Kansas, January 11, 1883
    d. January 22, 1962
    Governor of South Dakota, 1943-47

SHELDON, Charles H.
    Republican
    Governor of South Dakota, 1893-97

STERLING, Thomas
    Republican
    b. near Amanda, Ohio, February 21, 1851
    d. Washington, D. C., August 26, 1930
    U. S. Senator, 1913-15

VESSEY, Robert Scadder
    Republican
    b. near Oshkosh, Wis., May 16, 1858
    d. ----
    Governor of South Dakota, 1909-13

WERNER, Theodore B.
    Democrat
    b. Ossian, Iowa, June 2, 1892
    U. S. Representative, 1933-37

WILLIAMSON, William
    Republican
    b. near New Sharon, Iowa, October 7, 1875
    U. S. Representative, 1921-33

PROMINENT PERSONALITIES

The following select list of prominent persons of South Dakota has been selected to indicate the valuable contributions they have made to American life.

BEADLE, William H. H.
    b. January 1, 1838
    d. November 13, 1915
    Superintendent Public Instruction, Dakota
        Territory, 1879-85
    Leader of statehood movement
    President, Madison State Normal School,
        1889-1905
    Author: *Geography, History and Resources
        of Dakota Territory*, 1888
            *The Natural System of Teaching
        Geography*, 1899

CLARK, Charles Badger
    b. Albia, Iowa, January 1, 1883
    d. September 26, 1957
    Poet Laureate of South Dakota
    Author: *Sun and Saddle Leather*, 1915
            Grass Grown Trails, 1917
            Sky Lines and Wood Smoke, 1935
            Novel - *Spike*, 1923

HARE, William Hobart
    b. Princeton, N. J., 1838
    d. 1909
    Bishop of Niobrara, 1873-1909
        Bishopric enlarged, 1883 - made co-
        terminous with newly created Terri-
        tory of S. D., renamed South Dakota

HUMPHREY, Hubert Horatio, Jr.
    b. Wallace, S. D., May 27, 1911
    d. ----
    Pharmacist with Humphrey Drug Co., Huron,
        S. D., 1933-37
    Mayor of Minneapolis, 1945-48
    U. S. Senator, 1949-64
    U. S. Vice President, 1965-69
    U. S. Senator, 1971-78

LAWRENCE, Ernest O.
    b. Canton, S. C., August 8, 1901
    d. August 27, 1958
    Professor of Physics, University of California,
        1930-58
    Director of Radiation Laboratory, 1936
    Recipient Nobel Prize for Physics, 1939
    Awarded Medal for Merit, 1946

SITTING BULL
    b. 1831

d. Grand River, December 15, 1890
Became head of Strong Heart Warrior Society, 1856
Became Chief of Northern Hunting Sioux, 1866
Accepted peace-guaranteed reservation north of North Platte River, 1868
Became head of Sioux Confederacy War Council, 1875
Surrendered, July 1881

WARD, Joseph
b. Perry Centre, N. Y., May 5, 1838
d. December 11, 1889
Missionary in Dakota Territory
Established school which became first public high school in Dakota
Founded Yankton College, first college in upper Mississippi, Valley - first president, 1881-89

FIRST STATE CONSTITUTION

PROCLAMATION ANNOUNCING ADMISSION OF SOUTH DAKOTA—
1889

By the President of the United States of America

A PROCLAMATION

Whereas the Congress of the United States did, by an act approved on the twenty-second day of February, one thousand eight hundred and eighty-nine, provide that the inhabitants of the Territory of Dakota might, upon the conditions prescribed in the said act, become the States of North Dakota and South Dakota;

And whereas it was provided by said act that the area comprising the Territory of Dakota should, for the purposes of the act, be divided on the line of the seventh standard parallel produced due west to the western boundary of said Territory, and that the delegates elected as therein provided to the Constitutional convention in districts south of said parallel should, at the time prescribed in the act, assemble in convention at the city of Sioux Falls;

And whereas it was provided by the said act that the delegates elected as aforesaid should, after they had met and organized, declare on behalf of the people of South Dakota that they adopt the Constitution of the United States; whereupon the said convention should be authorized to form a constitution and State Government for the proposed State of South Dakota;

And whereas it was provided by said act that the constitution so adopted should be republican in form, and make no distinction in civil or political rights on account of race or color, except as to Indians not taxed, and not be repugnant to the Constitution of the United States and the principles of the Declaration of Independence;

and that the convention should, by an ordinance irrevocable without the consent of the United States and the people of said States, make certain provisions prescribed in said act;

And whereas it was provided by said act that the constitutions of North Dakota and South Dakota should, respectively, incorporate an agreement to be reached in accordance with the provisions of the act, for an equitable division of all property belonging to the Territory of Dakota, the disposition of all public records, and also for the apportionment of the debts and liabilities of said Territory, and that each of said States should obligate itself to pay its proportion of such debts and liabilities the same as if they had been created by such States respectively;

And whereas it was provided by said act that at the election for delegates to the constitutional convention in South Dakota, as therein provided, each elector might have written or printed on his ballot the words "For the Sioux Falls constitution," or the words "against the Sioux Falls constitution;" that the votes on this question should be returned and canvassed in the same manner as the votes for the election of delegates; and, if a majority of all votes cast on this question should be "for the Sioux Falls constitution" it should be the duty of the convention which might assemble at Sioux Falls, as provided in the act, to re-submit to the people of South Dakota, for ratification or rejection, at an election provided for in said act, the constitution framed at Sioux Falls and adopted November third, eighteen hundred and eighty-five, and also the articles and propositions separately submitted at that election, including the question of locating the temporary seat of government, with such changes only as related to the name and boundary of the proposed State, to the reapportionment of the judicial and legislative districts, and such amendments as might be necessary in order to comply with the provisions of the act;

And whereas it was provided by said act that the constitution formed for the people of South Dakota should, by an ordinance of the convention forming the same, be submitted to the people of South Dakota at an election to be held therein on the first Tuesday in October, eighteen hundred and eighty-nine, for ratification or rejection by the qualified voters of said proposed State, and that the returns of said election should be made to the Secretary of the Territory of Dakota, who, with the Governor and Chief Justice thereof, or any two of them, should canvass the same, and if a majority of the legal votes cast should be for the constitution the Governor should certify the result to the President of the United States, together with a statement of the votes cast thereon and upon separate articles or propositions, and a copy of said constitution, articles, propositions and ordinances;

And whereas it has been certified to me by the Governor of the Territory of Dakota that at the aforesaid election for delegates the "Sioux Falls constitution" was submitted to the people of the proposed State of South Dakota, as provided in the said act; that a majority of all the votes cast on this question was "for the Sioux Falls constitution;" and that the said constitution was, at the time prescribed in the act resubmittted to the people of South Dakota, with proper changes and amendments, and has been adopted and ratified by a majority of the qualified voters of said proposed State, in accordance with the conditions prescribed in said act;

And whereas it is also certified to me by the said Governor that at the same time that the body of said Constitution was submitted to a vote of the people, two additional articles were submitted separately to wit: an article numbered twenty-four entitled "Prohibition," which received a majority of all the votes cast for and against said article, as well as a majority of all the votes cast for and against the constitution and was adopted; and an article numbered twenty-five, entitled "Minority Representation," which did not receive a majority of the votes cast thereon or upon the constitution and was rejected;

And whereas a duly authenticated copy of said constitution, additional articles, ordinances and propositions as required by said act, has been received by me:

Now, therefore, I, Benjamin Harrison, President of the United States of America, do, in accordance with the act of Congress aforesaid, declare and proclaim the fact that the conditions imposed by Congress on the State of South Dakota to entitle that State to admission to the Union have been ratified and accepted, and that the admission of the said State into the Union is now complete.

In testimony whereof, I have hereunto set my hand and caused the seal of the United States to be affixed.

Done at the City of Washington this second day of November in the year of our Lord one thousand eight hundred and [SEAL.] eighty-nine, and of the Independence of the United States of America the one hundred and fourteenth.

BENJ. HARRISON.

By the President:
  JAMES G. BLAINE,
    Secretary of State.

CONSTITUTION OF SOUTH DAKOTA—1889 *[a]

PREAMBLE

We, the people of South Dakota, grateful to Almighty God for our civil and religious liberties, in order to form a more perfect and independent government, establish justice, insure tranquility, provide for the common defense, promote the general welfare and preserve to ourselves and to our posterity the blessings of liberty, do ordain and establish this constitution for the State of South Dakota.

---

* Verified from "The Enabling Act and Constitution of South Dakota. Constitution Adopted October 1, 1889. Free Press Company, Legal Blank and Law Publishers, Pierre, S. D." LXXIX pp.

Also the Revised Codes of South Dakota, 1903, pp. 1–26; also, Laws Passed at the Ninth Session of the Legislature of South Dakota, Aberdeen, S. D.: 1905. (Constitution as amended.)

See also the Constitution of the United States, Constitution of South Dakota, and Enabling Act admitting South Dakota. Hipple Printing Co. 1904. 31 pp.

[a] Adopted by popular vote October 1, 1889. Yeas, 70,131; nays, 3,267.

Article I

NAME AND BOUNDARY

§ 1. The name of the State shall be South Dakota.

§ 2. The boundaries of the State of South Dakota shall be as follows: Beginning at the point of intersection of the western boundary line of the State of Minnesota with the northern boundary line of the State of Iowa, and running thence northerly along the western boundary line of the State of Minnesota to its intersection with the 7th standard parallel; thence west on the line of the 7th standard parallel produced due west to its intersection with the 27th meridian of longitude west from Washington; thence south on the 27th meridian of longitude west from Washington to its intersection with the northern boundary line of the State of Nebraska; thence easterly along the northern boundary line of the State of Nebraska to its intersection with the western boundary line of the State of Iowa; thence northerly along the western boundary line of the State of Iowa to its intersection with the northern boundary line of the State of Iowa; thence east along the northern boundary line of the State of Iowa to the place of beginning.

Article II

DIVISION OF THE POWERS OF GOVERNMENT

The powers of the government of the state are divided into three distinct departments—the legislative, executive and judicial; and the powers and duties of each are prescribed by this constitution.

Article III

LEGISLATIVE DEPARTMENT

[a] § 1. The legislative power shall be vested in a legislature, which shall consist of a senate and house of representatives.

§ 2. The number of members of the house of representatives shall not be less than seventy-five nor more than one hundred and thirty-five. The number of members of the senate shall not be less than twenty-five nor more than forty-five.

The sessions of the legislature shall be biennial except as otherwise provided in this constitution.

§ 3. No person shall be eligible to the office of senator who is not a qualified elector in the district from which he may be chosen, and a citizen of the United States, and who shall not have attained the age of twenty-five years, and who shall not have been a resident of the state or territory for two years next preceding his election.

No person shall be eligible to the office of representative who is not a qualified elector in the district from which he may be chosen, and a citizen of the United States, and who shall not have been a resident of the state or territory for two years next preceding his election, and who shall not have attained the age of twenty-five years.

---

[a] See amendment, 1898.

No judge or clerk of any court, secretary of state, attorney general, state's attorney, recorder, sheriff or collector of public moneys, member of either house of congress, or person holding any lucrative office under the United States or this state, or any foreign government, shall be a member of the legislature; *Provided*, that appointments in the militia, the offices of notary public and justice of the peace shall not be considered lucrative; nor shall any person holding any office of honor or profit under any foreign government or under the government of the United States, except postmasters whose annual compensation does not exceed the sum of three hundred dollars, hold any office in either branch of the legislature or become a member thereof.

§ 4. No person who has been, or hereafter shall be, convicted of bribery, perjury or other infamous crime, nor any person who has been, or may be collector or holder of public moneys who shall not have accounted for and paid over, according to law, all such moneys due from him, shall be eligible to the legislature or to any office in either branch thereof.

§ 5. The legislature shall provide by law for the enumeration of the inhabitants of the state in the year one thousand eight hundred and ninety-five and every ten years thereafter, and at its first regular session after each enumeration, and also after each enumeration made by authority of the United States, but at no other time, the legislature shall apportion the senators and representatives according to the number of inhabitants, excluding Indians not taxed and soldiers and officers of the United States army and navy; *Provided*, that the legislature may make an apportionment at its first session after the admission of South Dakota as a State.

§ 6. The terms of the office of the members of the legislature shall be two years; they shall receive for their services the sum of five dollars for each day's attendance during the session of the legislature, and five [a] cents for every mile of necessary travel in going to and returning from the place of meeting of the legislature on the most usual route.

Each regular session of the legislature shall not exceed sixty days, except in cases of impeachment, and members of the legislature shall receive no other pay or perquisites except per diem and mileage.

§ 7. The legislature shall meet at the seat of government on the first Tuesday after the first Monday of January at 12 o'clock M., in the year next ensuing the election of members thereof, and at no other time except as provided by this constitution.

§ 8. Members of the legislature and officers thereof, before they enter upon their official duties, shall take and subscribe the following oath or affirmation: I do solemnly swear (or affirm) that I will support the constitution of the United States and the constitution of the State of South Dakota, and will faithfully discharge the duties of (senator, representative or officer) according to the best of my abilities, and that I have not knowingly or intentionally paid or contributed anything, or made any promise in the nature of a bribe, to directly or indirectly influence any vote at the election at which I

---

[a] The mileage of members of the legislature was amended by reducing from "ten" to "five" cents per mile, by popular vote of 39,364 for and 11,236 against, at the general election of 1892.

was chosen to fill said office, and have not accepted, nor will I accept or receive, directly or indirectly, any money, pass, or any other valuable thing, from any corporation, company or person, for any vote or influence I may give or withhold on any bill or resolution, or appropriation, or for any other official act.

This oath shall be administered by a judge of the supreme or circuit court, or the presiding officer of either house, in the hall of the house to which the member or officer is elected, and the secretary of state shall record and file the oath subscribed by each member and officer.

Any member or officer of the legislature who shall refuse to take the oath herein prescribed shall forfeit his office.

Any member or officer of the legislature who shall be convicted of having sworn falsely to or violated his said oath, shall forfeit his office and be disqualified thereafter from holding the office of senator or member of the house of representatives or any office within the gift of the legislature.

§ 9. Each house shall be the judge of the election returns and qualifications of its own members.

A majority of the members of each house shall constitute a quorum, but a smaller number may adjourn from day to day, and may compel the attendance of absent members in such a manner and under such penalty as each house may provide.

Each house shall determine the rules of its proceedings, shall choose its own officers and employes and fix the pay thereof, except as otherwise provided in this constitution.

§ 10. The governor shall issue writs of election to fill such vacancies as may occur in either house of the legislature.

§ 11. Senators and representatives shall, in all cases except treason, felony or breach of the peace, be privileged from arrest during the session of the legislature, and in going to and returning from the same; and for words used in any speech or debate in either house, they shall not be questioned in any other place.

§ 12. No member of the legislature shall, during the term for which he was elected, be appointed or elected to any civil office in the State which shall have been created, or the emoluments of which shall have been increased during the term for which he was elected, nor shall any member receive any civil appointment from the governor, the governor and senate, or from the legislature during the term for which he shall have been elected, and all such appointments and all votes given for any such members for any such office or appointment shall be void; nor shall any member of the legislature during the term for which he shall have been elected, or within one year thereafter, be interested, directly or indirectly, in any contract with the State or any county thereof, authorized by any law passed during the term for which he shall have been elected.

§ 13. Each house shall keep a journal of its proceedings and publish the same from time to time, except such parts as require secrecy, and the yeas and nays of members on any question shall be taken at the desire of one-sixth of those present and entered upon the journal.

§ 14. In all elections to be made by the legislature the members thereof shall vote *viva voce* and their votes shall be entered in the journal.

§ 15. The sessions of each house and of the committee of the whole shall be open, unless when the business is such as ought to be kept secret.

§ 16. Neither house shall, without the consent of the other, adjourn for more than three days, nor to any other place than that in which the two houses shall be sitting.

§ 17. Every bill shall be read three several times, but the first and second reading may be on the same day, and the second reading may be by the title of the bill, unless the reading at length be demanded. The first and third readings shall be at length.

§ 18. The enacting clause of a law shall be: " Be it enacted by the Legislature of the State of South Dakota," and no law shall be passed unless by assent of a majority of all the members elected to each house of the legislature. And the question upon the final passage shall be taken upon its last reading, and the yeas and nays shall be entered upon the journal.

§ 19. The presiding officer of each house shall, in the presence of the house over which he presides, sign all bills and joint resolutions passed by the legislature, after their titles have been publicly read immediately before signing, and the fact of signing shall be entered upon the journal.

§ 20. Any bill may originate in either house of the legislature, and a bill passed by one house may be amended in the other.

§ 21. No law shall embrace more than one subject, which shall be expressed in its title.

§ 22. No act shall take effect until ninety days after the adjournment of the session at which it passed, unless in case of emergency (to be expressed in the preamble or body of the act) the legislature shall, by a vote of two-thirds of all the members elected of each house, otherwise direct.

§ 23. The legislature is prohibited from enacting any private or special laws in the following cases:

1. Granting divorces.
2. Changing the names of persons or places, or constituting one person the heir-at-law of another.
3. Locating or changing county-seats.
4. Regulating county and township affairs.
5. Incorporating cities, towns and villages or changing or amending the charter of any town, city or village, or laying out, opening, vacating or altering town plats, streets, wards, alleys and public grounds.
6. Providing for sale or mortgage of real estate belonging to minors or others under disability.
7. Authorizing persons to keep ferries across streams wholly within the State.
8. Remitting fines, penalties or forfeitures.
9. Granting to an individual, association or corporation any special or exclusive privilege, immunity or franchise whatever.
10. Providing for the management of common schools.
11. Creating, increasing or decreasing fees, percentages or allowances of public officers during the term for which said officers are elected or appointed.

But the legislature may repeal any existing special law relating to the foregoing subdivisions.

In all other cases where a general law can be applicable, no special law shall be enacted.

§ 24. The legislature shall have no power to release or extinguish, in whole or in part, the indebtedness, liability or obligation of any corporation or individual to this State or to any municipal corporation therein.

§ 25. The legislature shall not authorize any game of chance, lottery or gift enterprise, under any pretense, or for any purpose whatever.

§ 26. The legislature shall not delegate to any special commission, private corporation or association any power to make, supervise or interfere with any municipal improvement, money, property, effects, whether held in trust or otherwise, or levy taxes or to select a capital site or to perform any municipal functions whatever.

§ 27. The legislature shall direct by law in what manner and in what court suits may be brought against the State.

§ 28. Any person who shall give, demand, offer, directly or indirectly, any money, testimonial, privilege or personal advantage, anything of value to an executive or judicial officer or member of the legislature, to influence him in the performance of any of his official or public duties shall be guilty of bribery and shall be punished in such manner as shall be provided by law.

The offense of corrupt solicitation of members of the legislature, or of public officers of the State, or any municipal division thereof, and any effort toward solicitation of said members of the legislature or officers to influence their official action shall be defined by law, and shall be punishable by fine and imprisonment.

Any person may be compelled to testify in investigation or judicial proceedings against any person charged with having committed any offense of bribery or corrupt solicitation, and shall not be permitted to withhold his testimony upon the ground that it may criminate himself, but said testimony shall not afterward be used against him in any judicial proceeding except for bribery in giving such testimony, and any person convicted of either of the offenses aforesaid shall be disqualified from holding any office or position or office of trust or profit in this State.

Article IV

EXECUTIVE DEPARTMENT

§ 1. The executive power shall be vested in a governor who shall hold his office for two years. A lieutenant governor shall be elected at the same time and for the same term.

§ 2. No person shall be eligible to the office of governor or lieutenant governor except a citizen of the United States and a qualified elector of the State, who shall have attained the age of 30 years, and who shall have resided two years next preceding the election within the State or territory; nor shall he be eligible to any other office during the term for which he shall have been elected.

§ 3. The governor and lieutenant governor shall be elected by the qualified electors of the State at the time and places of choosing members of the legislature. The persons respectively having the highest number of votes for governor and lieutenant governor shall be elected; but if two or more shall have an equal and highest number of votes for governor or lieutenant governor, the two houses of the legislature at its next regular session shall forthwith, by joint ballot, choose one of such persons for said office. The returns of the election for governor and lieutenant governor shall be made in such manner as shall be prescribed by law.

§ 4. The governor shall be commander-in-chief of the military and naval forces of the State, except when they shall be called into the service of the United States, and may call out the same to execute laws, suppress insurrection and repel invasion. He shall have power to convene the legislature on extraordinary occasions. He shall, at the commencement of each session, communicate to the legislature by message, information of the condition of the State, and shall recommend such measures as he shall deem expedient. He shall transact all necessary business with the officers of the government, civil and military. He shall expedite all such measures as may be resolved upon by the legislature and shall take care that the laws be faithfully executed.

§ 5. The governor shall have power to remit fines and forfeitures, to grant reprieves, commutations and pardons after conviction for all offences except treason and cases of impeachment; provided, that in all cases where the sentence of the court is capital punishment, imprisonment for life or a longer term than two years, or a fine exceeding $200, no pardon shall be granted, sentence commuted or fine remitted except upon the recommendation in writing of a board of pardons, consisting of the presiding judge, secretary of state and attorney general, after full hearing in open session, and such recommendation, with the reasons therefor, shall be filed in the office of the secretary of state; but the legislature may by law in all cases regulate the manner in which the remission of fines, pardons, commutations and reprieves may be applied for. Upon conviction for treason he shall have the power to suspend the execution of the sentence until the case shall be reported to the legislature at its next regular session, when the legislature shall either pardon or commute the sentence, direct the execution of the sentence or grant a further reprieve. He shall communicate to the legislature at each regular session, each case of remission of fine, reprieve, commutation or pardon granted by him in the cases in which he is authorized to act without the recommendation of the said board of pardons, stating the name of the convict, the crime of which he is convicted, the sentence and its date, and the date of the remission, commutation, pardon or reprieve, with his reasons for granting the same.

§ 6. In case of death, impeachment, resignation, failure to qualify, absence from the State, removal from office, or other disability of the governor, the powers and duties of the office for the residue of the term, or until he shall be acquitted, or the disability removed, shall devolve upon the lieutenant governor.

§ 7. The lieutenant governor shall be president of the senate, but shall have only a casting vote therein. If during a vacancy of the office of governor the lieutenant governor shall be impeached, displaced, resign or die, or from mental or physical disease or otherwise become incapable of performing the duties of his office the secretary of state shall act as governor until the vacancy shall be filled or the disability removed.

§ 8. When any office shall from any cause become vacant and no mode is provided by the constitution or law for filling such vacancy, the governor shall have the power to fill such vacancy by appointment.

§ 9. Every bill which shall have passed the legislature shall, before it becomes a law, be presented to the governor. If he approve, he shall sign it; but if not, he shall return it with his objection to the house in which it originated, which shall enter the objection at large upon the journal and proceed to reconsider it. If after such reconsideration, two-thirds of the members present shall agree to pass the bill, it shall be sent together with the objection, to the other house, by which it shall likewise be reconsidered, and if it be approved by two-thirds of the members present, it shall become a law; but in all such cases the vote of both houses shall be determined by the yeas and nays, and the names of the members voting for and against the bill shall be entered upon the journal of each house respectively. If any bill shall [not] be returned by the governor within three days (Sundays excepted) after it shall have been presented to him, the same shall be a law, unless the legislature shall by its adjournment prevent its return, in which case it shall be filed, with his objection, in the office of the secretary of state within ten days after such adjournment, or become a law.

§ 10. The governor shall have power to disapprove of any item or items of any bill making appropriations of money embracing distinct items, and the part or parts of the bill approved shall be law, and the item or items disapproved shall be void, unless enacted in the following manner: If the legislature be in session he shall transmit to the house in which the bill originated, a copy of the item or items thereof disapproved, together with his objections thereto, and the items objected to shall be separately reconsidered, and each item shall then take the same course as is prescribed for the passage of bills over the executive veto.

§ 11. Any governor of this State who asks, receives, or agrees to receive any bribe upon any understanding that his official opinion, judgment or action shall be influenced thereby, or who gives or offers, or promises his official influence in consideration that any member of the legislature shall give his official vote or influence on any particular side of any question or matter upon which he may be required to act in his official capacity, or who menaces any member by the threatened use of his veto power or who offers or promises any member that he, the said governor, will appoint any particular person or persons to any office created or thereafter to be created in consideration that any member shall give his official vote or influence on any matter pending or thereafter to be introduced into either house of said legislature or who threatenes any member that he, the said governor, will remove any person or persons from any office or position with intent to in any manner influence the official action of said member, shall be punished in the manner now, or that may hereafter be, provided by law, and upon conviction thereon shall forfeit all right to hold or exercise any office of trust or honor in this State.

§ 12. There shall be chosen by the qualified electors of the State at the times and places of choosing members of the legislature, a secretary of state, auditor, treasurer, superintendent of public instruction, commissioner of school and public lands, and attorney general, who shall severally hold their offices for the term of two years, but no person shall be eligible to the office of treasurer for more than two terms consectively. They shall respectively keep their offices at the seat of government.

§ 13. The powers and duties of the secretary of state, auditor, treasurer, superintendent of public instruction, commissioner of school and public lands and attorney general shall be as prescribed by law.

Article V

JUDICIAL DEPARTMENT

§ 1. The judicial powers of the State, except as in this constitution otherwise provided, shall be vested in a supreme court, circuit courts, county courts and justices of the peace, and such other courts as may be created by law for cities and incorporated towns.

SUPREME COURT

§ 2. The supreme court, except as otherwise provided in this constitution, shall have appellate jurisdiction only, which shall be co-extensive with the State, and shall have a general superintending control over all inferior courts, under such regulations and limitations as may be prescribed by law.

§ 3. The supreme court and the judges thereof shall have power to issue writs of habeas corpus. The supreme court shall have power to issue writs of mandamus, quo warranto, certiorari, injunction and other original and remedial writs, with authority to hear and determine the same in such cases and under such regulations as may be prescribed by law, provided, however, that no jury trials shall be allowed in said supreme court, but, in proper cases, questions of fact may be sent by said court to a circuit court for a trial before a jury.

§ 4. At least two terms of the supreme court shall be held each year at the seat of government.

§ 5. The supreme court shall consist of three judges, to be chosen from districts by qualified electors of the State at large, as hereinafter provided.

§ 6. The number of said judges and districts may, after five years from the admission of this State under this constitution, be increased by law to not exceeding five.

§ 7. A majority of the judges of the supreme court shall be necessary to form a quorum or to pronounce a decision, but one or more of said judges may adjourn the court from day to day or to a day certain.

§ 8. The term of the judges of the supreme court who shall be elected at the first election under this constitution shall be four years. At all subsequent elections the term of said judges shall be six years.

§ 9. The judges of the supreme court shall by rules select from their number a presiding judge, who shall act as such for the term prescribed by such rule.

§ 10. No person shall be eligible to the office of judge of the supreme court unless he be learned in the law, be at least thirty years of age, a citizen of the United States, nor unless he shall have resided in this State or territory at least two years next preceding his election and at the time of his election be a resident of the district from which he is elected; but for the purpose of re-election, no such judge shall be deemed to have lost his residence in the district by reason of his removal to the seat of government in the discharge of his official duties.

§ 11. Until otherwise provided by law, the districts from which the said judges of the supreme court shall be elected shall be constituted as follows:

First District—All that portion of the State lying west of the Missouri river.

Second District—All that portion of the State lying east of the Missouri river and south of the second standard parallel.

Third District—All that portion of the State lying east of the Missouri river and north of the second standard parallel.

§ 12. There shall be a clerk and also a reporter of the supreme court, who shall be appointed by the judges thereof and who shall hold office during the pleasure of said judges, and whose duties and emoluments shall be prescribed by law, and by the rules of the supreme court not inconsistent with law. The legislature shall make provisions for the publication and distribution of the decisions of the supreme court, and for the sale of the published volumes thereof. No private person or corporation shall be allowed to secure any copyright to such decisions, but if any copyrights are secured they shall innure wholly to the benefit of the State.

§ 13. The governor shall have authority to require the opinions of the judges of the supreme court upon important questions of law involved in the exercise of his executive powers and upon solemn occasions.

CIRCUIT COURTS

§ 14. The circuit courts shall have original jurisdiction of all actions and causes, both at law and in equity, and such appellate jurisdiction as may be conferred by law and consistent with this constitution; such jurisdiction as to value and amount and grade of offense, may be limited by law. They and the judges thereof shall also have jurisdiction and power to issue writs of habeas corpus, mandamus, quo warranto, certiorari, injunction and other original and remedial writs, with authority to hear and determine the same.

§ 15. The state shall be divided into judicial circuits in each of which there shall be elected by the electors thereof one judge of the circuit court therein, whose term of office shall be four years.

§ 16. Until otherwise ordered by law, said circuits shall be eight in number and constituted as follows, viz:

First Circuit—The counties of Union, Clay, Yankton, Turner, Bon Homme, Hutchinson, Charles Mix, Douglas, Todd, Gregory, Tripp. and Meyer.

Second Circuit—The counties of Lincoln, Minnehaha, McCook, Moody and Lake.

Third Circuit—The counties of Brookings, Kingsbury, Deuel,

Hamlin, Codington, Clark, Grant, Roberts, Day, and the Wahpeton and Sisseton reservation, except such portion of such reservation as lies in Marshall county.

Fourth Circuit—The counties of Sanborn, Davison, Aurora, Brule, Buffalo, Jerauld, Hanson, Miner, Lyman, Presho and Pratt.

Fifth Circuit—The counties of Beadle, Spink, Brown and Marshall.

Sixth Circuit—The counties of Hand, Hyde, Hughes, Sully, Stanley, Potter, Faulk, Edmunds, Walworth, Campbell and McPherson and all that portion of said state lying east of the Missouri river and not included in any other judicial circuit.

Seventh Circuit—The counties of Pennington, Custer, Fall River, Shannon, Washington, Ziebach, Sterling, Nowlin, Jackson, Washabaugh and Lugenbeel.

Eighth Circuit—The counties of Lawrence, Meade, Scobey, Butte, Delano, Pyatt, Dewey, Boreman, Schnasse, Rinehart, Martin, Choteau, Ewing and Harding and all that portion of said state west of the Missouri river and north of the Big Cheyenne river and the north fork of the Cheyenne river not included in any other judicial circuit.

§ 17. The legislature may, whenever two-thirds of the members of each house shall concur therein, increase the number of judicial circuits and the judges thereof, and divide the State into judicial circuits accordingly, taking care that they be formed of compact territory and be bounded by county lines, but such increase of number or change in the boundaries of districts shall not work the removal of any judge from his office during the term for which he shall have been elected or appointed.

§ 18. Writs of error and appeals may be allowed from the decisions of the circuit courts to the supreme court under such regulations as may be prescribed by law.

COUNTY COURTS

§ 19. There shall be elected in each organized county a county judge who shall be judge of the county court of said county, whose term of office shall be two years until otherwise provided by law.

§ 20. County courts shall be courts of record and shall have original jurisdiction in all matters of probate guardianship and settlement of estates of deceased persons, and such other civil and criminal jurisdiction as may be conferred by law; *Provided*, that such courts shall not have jurisdiction in any case where the debt, damage, claim or value of property involved shall exceed one thousand dollars except in matters of probate, guardianship and the estates of deceased persons. Writs of error and appeal may be allowed from county to circuit courts, or to the supreme court, in such cases and in such manner as may be prescribed by law; *Provided*, that no appeal or writ of error shall be allowed to the circuit court from any judgment rendered upon an appeal from a justice of the peace or police magistrate for cities or towns.

§ 21. The county court shall not have jurisdiction in cases of felony, nor shall criminal cases therein be prosecuted by indictment; but they may have such jurisdiction in criminal matters, not of the grade of felony, as the legislature may prescribe, and the prosecutions therein may be by information or otherwise as the legislature may provide.

JUSTICE OF THE PEACE

§ 22. Justices of the peace shall have such jurisdiction as may be conferred by law, but they shall not have jurisdiction of any cause wherein the value of the property or the amount in controversy exceeds the sum of one hundred dollars, or where the boundaries or title to real property shall be called in question.

POLICE MAGISTRATE

§ 23. The legislature shall have power to provide for creating such police magistrates for cities and towns as may be deemed from time to time necessary, who shall have jurisdiction of all cases arising under the ordinances of such cities and towns respectively, and such police magistrates may also be constituted ex-officio justices of the peace for their respective counties.

STATE'S ATTORNEY

§ 24. The legislature shall have power to provide for State's attorneys and to prescribe their duties and fix their compensation; but no person shall be eligible to the office of attorney general or State's attorney who shall not at the time of his election be at least 25 years of age and possess all the other qualifications for judges of circuit courts as prescribed in this article.

MISCELLANEOUS

§ 25. No person shall be eligible to the office of judge of the circuit or county courts unless he be learned in the law, be at least 25 years of age, and a citizen of the United States; nor unless he shall have resided in this state or territory at least one year next preceding his election, and at the time of his election be a resident of the county or circuit, as the case may be, for which he is elected.

§ 26. The judges of the supreme court, circuit courts and county courts shall be chosen at the first election held under the provisions of this constitution, and thereafter as provided by law, and the legislature may provide for the election of such officers on a different day from that on which an election is held for any other purpose and may, for the purpose of making such provision, extend or abridge the term of office for any such judges, then holding, but not in any case more than six months. The term of office of all judges of circuit courts, elected in the several judicial circuits throughout the state, shall expire on the same day.

§ 27. The time of holding courts within said judicial circuits and counties shall be as provided by law; but at least one term of the circuit court shall be held annually in each organized county, and the legislature shall make provision for attaching unorganized counties or territory to original counties for judicial purposes.

§ 28. Special terms of said courts may be held under such regulations as may be provided by law.

§ 29. The judges of the circuit courts may hold courts in other circuits than their own under such regulations as may be prescribed by law.

§ 30. The judges of the supreme court, circuit courts and county courts shall each receive such salary as may be provided by law, consistent with this constitution, and no such judge shall receive any compensation, perquisite or emoluments for or on account of his office in any form whatever except such salary; provided that county judges may accept and receive such fees as may be allowed under the land laws of the United States.

§ 31. No judge of the supreme court or circuit court shall act as attorney or counselor at law, nor shall any county judge act as an attorney or counselor at law in any case which is or may be brought into his court, or which may be appealed therefrom.

§ 32. There shall be a clerk of the circuit court in each organized county who shall also be clerk of the county court, and who shall be elected by the qualified electors of such county. The duties and compensation of said clerk shall be as provided by law and regulated by the rules of the court consistent with the provisions of law.

§ 33. Until the legislature shall provide by law for fixing the terms of courts, the judges of the supreme, circuit and county courts respectively shall fix the terms thereof.

§ 34. All laws relating to courts shall be general and of uniform operation throughout the state, and the organization, jurisdiction, power, proceedings and practice of all the courts of the same class or grade, so far as regulated by law, and the force and effect of the proceedings, judgments and decrees of such courts severally shall be uniform; *Provided, however*, that the legislature may classify the county courts according to the population of the respective counties and fix the jurisdiction and salary of the judges thereof, accordingly.

§ 35. No judge of the supreme or circuit courts shall be elected to any other than a judicial office or be eligible thereto, during the term for which he was elected such judge. All votes for either of them during such term for any elective office, except that of judge of the supreme court, circuit court or county court, given by the legislature or the people, shall be void.

§ 36. All judges or other officers of the supreme, circuit or county courts provided for in this article shall hold their offices until their successors respectively are elected or appointed and qualified.

§ 37. All officers provided for in this article shall respectively reside in the district, county, precinct, city or town for which they may be elected or appointed. Vacancies in the elective offices provided for in this article shall be filled by appointment until the next general election as follows: All judges of the supreme, circuit and county courts by the governor. All other judicial and other officers by the county board of the counties where the vacancy occurs; in cases of police magistrates, by the municipality.

§ 38. All process shall run in the name of the "State of South Dakota." All prosecutions shall be carried on in the name of and by authority of the "State of South Dakota."

Article VI

BILL OF RIGHTS

§ 1. All men are born equally free and independent, and have certain inherent rights, among which are those of enjoying and defending life and liberty, of acquiring and protecting property and the pursuit of happiness. To secure these rights governments are instituted among men, deriving their just powers from the consent of the governed.

§ 2. No person shall be deprived of life, liberty or property without due process of law.

§ 3. The right to worship God according to the dictates of conscience shall never be infringed. No person shall be denied any civil or political right, privilege or position on account of his religious opinions; but the liberty of conscience hereby secured shall not be so construed as to excuse licentiousness, the invasion of the rights of others, or justify practices inconsistent with the peace or safety of the State. No person shall be compelled to attend or support any ministry or place of worship against his consent, nor shall any preference be given by law to any religious establishment or mode of worship. No money or property of the state shall be given or appropriated for the benefit of any sectarian or religious society or institution.

§ 4. The right of petition, and of the people peaceably to assemble to consult for the common good and make known their opinions, shall never be abridged.

§ 5. Every person may freely speak, write and publish on all subjects, being responsible for the abuse of that right. In all trials for libel, both civil and criminal, the truth, when published, with good motives and for justifiable ends, shall be a sufficient defense. The jury shall have the right to determine the facts and the law under the direction of the court.

§ 6. The right of trial by jury shall remain inviolate, and shall extend to all cases at law without regard to the amount in controversy, but the legislature may provide for a jury of less than twelve in any court not a court of record, and for the decision of civil cases by three-fourths of the jury in any court.

§ 7. In all criminal prosecutions the accused shall have the right to defend in person and by counsel; to demand the nature and cause of the accusation against him; to have a copy thereof; to meet the witnesses against him face to face; to have compulsory process served for obtaining witnesses in his behalf, and to a speedy public trial by an impartial jury of the county or district in which the offense is alleged to have been committed.

§ 8. All persons shall be bailable by sufficient sureties, except for capital offenses when proof is evident or presumption great. The privilege of the writ of habeas corpus shall not be suspended, unless when in case of rebellion or invasion the public safety may require it.

§ 9. No person shall be compelled in any criminal case to give evidence against himself or be twice put in jeopardy for the same offense.

§ 10. No person shall be held for a criminal offense unless on the presentment or indictment of the grand jury, or information of the public prosecutor, except in cases of impeachment, in cases cognizable by county courts, by justices of the peace, and in cases arising in the army and navy, or in the militia when in actual service in time of war or public danger. *Provided,* that the grand jury may be modified or abolished by law.

§ 11. The right of the people to be secure in their persons, houses, papers and effects, against unreasonable searches and seizures, shall not be violated, and no warrant shall issued but upon probable cause supported by affidavit, particularly describing the place to be searched and the person or thing to be seized.

§ 12. No *ex post facto* law, or law imparing the obligation of contracts or making any irrevocable grant or privilege, franchise or immunity shall be passed.

§ 13. Private property shall not be taken for public use, or damaged, without just compensation as determined by a jury, which shall be paid as soon as it can be ascertained and before possession is taken. No benefit which may accrue to the owner as a result of an improvement made by any private corporation shall be considered in fixing the compensation for property taken or damaged. The fee of land taken for railroad tracks or other highways shall remain in such owners, subject to the use for which it is taken.

§ 14. No distinction shall ever be made by law between resident aliens and citizens in reference to the possession, enjoyment or descent of property.

§ 15. No person shall be imprisoned for debt arising out of or founded upon a contract.

§ 16. The military shall be in strict subordination to the civil power. No soldier in time of peace shall be quartered in any house without consent of the owner, nor in time of war except in the manner prescribed by law.

§ 17. No tax or duty shall be imposed without the consent of the people or their respresentatives in the legislature, and all taxation shall be equal and uniform.

§ 18. No law shall be passed granting to any citizen, class of citizens or corporation, privileges or immunities which upon the same terms shall not equally belong to all citizens or corporations.

§ 19. Elections shall be free and equal, and no power, civil or military, shall at any time interfere to prevent the free exercise of the right of suffrage. Soldiers in time of war may vote at their post of duty in or out of the state, under regulations to be prescribed by the legislature.

§ 20. All courts shall be open, and every man for an injury done him in his property, person or reputation, shall have remedy by due course of law, and right and justice administered without denial or delay.

§ 21. No power of suspending law shall be exercised, unless by the legislature or its authority.

§ 22. No person shall be attainted of treason or felony by the legislature.

§ 23. Excessive bail shall not be required, excessive fines imposed, nor cruel punishments inflicted.

§ 24. The right of the citizens to bear arms in defense of themselves and the state shall not be denied.

§ 25. Treason against the state shall consist only in levying war against it, or in adhering to its enemies, or in giving them aid and comfort. No person shall be convicted of treason unless on the testimony of two witnesses to the same overt act or confession in open court.

§ 26. All political power is inherent in the people and all free government is founded on their authority, and is instituted for their equal protection and benefit, and they have the right in lawful and constituted methods to alter or reform their forms of government in such manner as they may think proper. And the state of South Dakota is an inseparable part of the American Union, and the constitution of the United States is the supreme law of the land.

§ 27. The blessings of a free government can only be maintained by a firm adherence to justice, moderation, temperance, frugality and virtue, and by frequent recurrence to fundamental principles.

Article VII

ELECTIONS AND RIGHT OF SUFFRAGE

§ 1. Every male person resident of this State who shall be of the age of 21 years and upwards, not otherwise disqualified, belonging to either of the following classes, who shall be a qualified elector under the laws of the territory of Dakota at the date of the ratification of this constitution by the people, or who shall have resided in the United States one year, in this state six months, in the county thirty days and in the election precinct where he offers his vote ten days next preceding any election, shall be deemed a qualified elector at such election.

First. Citizens of the United States.

Second. Persons of foreign birth who shall have declared their intention to become citizens conformably to the laws of the United States upon the subject of naturalization.

*§ 2. The legislature shall at its first session after the admission of the state into the Union, submit to a vote of the electors of the state the following question to be voted upon at the next general election held thereafter, namely: " Shall the word ' male ' be stricken from the article of the constitution relating to elections and the right of suffrage." If a majority of the votes cast upon that question are in favor of striking out said word " male " it shall be stricken out and there shall thereafter be no distinction between males and females in the exercise of the right of suffrage at any election in this state.

§ 3. All votes shall be by ballot, but the legislature may provide for numbering ballots for the purpose of preventing and detecting fraud.

§ 4. All general elections shall be biennial.

§ 5. Electors shall in all cases except treason, felony or breach of the peace, be privileged from arrest during their attendance at elections and in going to and returning from the same. And no elector shall be obliged to do military duty on the days of election except in time of war or public danger.

§ 6. No elector shall be deemed to have lost his residence in this state by reason of his absence on business of the United States or of this state, or in the military or naval service of the United States.

§ 7. No soldier, seaman or marine in the army or navy of the United States shall be deemed a resident of this state in consequence of being stationed therein.

§ 8. No person under guardianship, *non compos mentis* or insane, shall be qualified to vote at any election, nor shall any person con-

---

*This question was submitted to the people at the election held in November, 1890, and was rejected by the following vote: For, 22,072; against, 45,682.

victed of treason or felony be qualified to vote at any election unless restored to civil rights.

§ 9. Any woman having the qualifications enumerated in Section 1, of this article, as to age, residence and citizenship, and including those now qualified by the laws of the territory, may vote at any election held solely for school purposes, and may hold any office in this state except as otherwise provided in this constitution.

Article VIII

EDUCATION AND SCHOOL LANDS

§ 1. The stability of a republican form of government depending on the morality and intelligence of the people, it shall be the duty of the legislature to establish and maintain a general and uniform system of public schools wherein tuition shall be without charge, and equally open to all; and to adopt all suitable means to secure to the people the advantages and opportunities of education.

§ 2. All proceeds of the sale of public lands that have heretofore been or may hereafter be given by the United States for the use of public schools in the State; all such per centum as may be granted by the United States on the sales of public lands; the proceeds of all property that shall fall to the State by escheat; the proceeds of all gifts or donations to the State for public schools or not otherwise appropriated by the terms of the gift; and all property otherwise acquired for public schools, shall be and remain a perpetual fund for the maintenance of public schools in the State. It shall be deemed a trust fund held by the State. The principal shall forever remain inviolate, and may be increased, but shall never be diminished, and the State shall make good all losses thereof which may in any manner occur.

§ 3. The interest and income of this fund, together with the net proceeds of all fines for violation of State laws and all other sums which may be added thereto by law, shall be faithfully used and applied each year for the benefit of the public schools of the State, and shall be for this purpose apportioned among and between all the several public school corporations of the State in proportion to the number of children in each of school age, as may be fixed by law; and no part of the fund, either principal or interest, shall ever be diverted, even temporarily, from this purpose or used for any other purpose whatever than the maintenance of public schools for the equal benefit of all the people of the State.

§ 4. After one year from the assembling of the first legislature, the lands granted to the State by the United States for the use of public schools may be sold upon the following conditions and no other: Not more than one-third of all such lands shall be sold within the first five years, and no more than two-thirds within the first fifteen years after the title thereto is vested in the State and the legislature shall, subject to the provisions of this article, provide for the sale of the same.

The commissioner of school and public lands, the State auditor and the county superintendent of schools of the counties severally, shall constitute boards of appraisal and shall appraise all school lands within the several counties which they may from time to time select and designate for sale, at their actual value under the terms of sale. They shall take care to first select and designate for sale the most valuable lands; and they shall ascertain all such lands as may be of special and peculiar value, other than agricultural, and cause the proper sub-division of the same in order that the largest price may be obtained therefor.

§ 5. No land shall be sold for less than the appraised value, and in no case for less than ten dollars an acre. The purchaser shall pay one-fourth of the price in cash, and the remaining three-fourths as follows: One-fourth in five years, one-fourth in ten years, and one-fourth in fifteen years; with interest thereon at the rate of not less than six per centum per annum, payable annually in advance, but all such subdivided lands may be sold for cash, provided that upon payment of the interest for one full year in advance, the balance of the purchase price may be paid at any time. All sales shall be at public auction to the highest bidder, after sixty day's advertisement of the same in a newspaper of general circulation in the vicinity of the lands to be sold, and one at the seat of government. Such lands as shall not have been specially subdivided shall be offered in tracts of not more than eighty acres, and those so subdivided in the smallest subdivisions. All lands designated for sale and not sold within four years after appraisal, shall be reappraised by the board of appraisal as hereinbefore provided before they are sold.

§ 6. All sales shall be conducted through the office of the commissioner of school and public lands as may be prescribed by law, and returns of all appraisals and sales shall be made to said office. No sale shall operate to convey any right or title to any lands for sixty days after the date thereof, nor until the same shall have received the approval of the governor in such form as may be provided by law. No grant or patent for any such lands shall issue until final payment be made.

§ 7. All lands, money or other property donated, granted, or received from the United States or any other source for a university, agricultural college, normal schools or other educational or charitable institution or purpose, and the proceeds of all such lands and other property so received from any source, shall be and remain perpetual funds, the interest and income of which, together with the rents of all such lands as may remain unsold, shall be inviolably appropriated and applied to the specific objects of the original grants or gifts. The principal of every such fund may be increased, but shall never be diminished, and the interest and income only shall be used. Every such fund shall be deemed a trust fund held by the state, and the state shall make good all losses therefrom that shall in any manner occur.

§ 8. All lands mentioned in the preceding section shall be appraised and sold in the same manner and by the same officers and boards under the same limitations and subject to all the conditions as to price, sale and approval provided above for the appraisal and sale of lands for the benefit of public schools, but a distinct and separate account shall be kept by the proper officers of each of such funds.

§ 9. No lands mentioned in this article shall be leased except for pasturage and meadow purposes and at public auction after notice as hereinbefore provided in case of sale and shall be offered in tracts not greater than one section. All rents shall be payable annually in advance, and no term of lease shall exceed five years, nor shall any lease be valid until it receives the approval of the governor.

§ 10. No claim to any public lands by any tresspasser thereon by reason of occupancy, cultivation or improvement thereof, shall ever be recognized; nor shall compensation ever be made on account of any improvements made by such trespasser.

^a § 11. The moneys of the permanent school and other educational funds shall be invested only in first mortgages upon good improved farm lands within this State as hereinafter provided, or in bonds of school corporations within the State, or in bonds of the United States, or of the State of South Dakota. The legislature shall provide by law the method of determining the amounts of said funds which shall be invested from time to time in such classes of securities respectively, taking care to secure continuous investments as far as possible.

All moneys of said funds which may from time to time be designated for investment in farm mortgages and in the bonds of school corporations shall for such purpose be divided among the organized counties of the State in proportion to population as nearly as provisions by law to secure continuous investments may permit. The several counties shall hold and manage the same as trust funds, and they shall be and remain responsible and accountable for the principal and interest of all such moneys received by them from the date of receipt until returned because not loaned; and in case of loss to any money so apportioned to any county, such county shall make the same good out of its common revenue. Counties shall invest said money in bonds of school corporations, or in first mortgages upon good improved farm lands within their limits respectively; but no farm loan shall exceed $500 to any one person, nor shall it exceed one-half the valuation of the lands as assessed for taxation, and the rate of interest shall not be less than 6 per centum per annum, and shall be such other and higher rate as the legislature may provide, and shall be payable semi-annually on the first days of January and July; provided, that whenever there are moneys of said funds in any county amounting to $1,000 that cannot be loaned according to the provisions of this section and any law pursuant thereto, the said sum may be returned to the state treasurer to be entrusted to some other county or counties, or otherwise invested under the provisions of this section.

Each county shall semi-annually, on the first day of January and July, render an account of the condition of the funds intrusted to it to the auditor of state, and at the same time pay to or account to the state treasurer for the interest due on all funds intrusted to it.

The legislature may provide by general law that counties may retain from interest collected in excess of six per centum per annum upon all said funds intrusted to them, not to exceed one per centum per annum. But no county shall be exempted from the obligation to make semi-annual payments to the state treasury of interest at the rate provided by law for such loans, except only said one per centum, and in no case shall the interest so to be paid be less than six per centum per annum.

The legislature shall provide by law for the safe investment of the permanent school and other educational funds, and for the prompt

---

^a See amendment, 1902.

collection of interest and income thereof, and to carry out the objects and provisions of this section.

§ 12. The governor may disapprove any sale, lease or investment other than such as are intrusted to the counties.

§ 13. All losses to the permanent school or other educational funds of this state which shall have been occasioned by the defalcation, negligence, mismanagement or fraud of the agents or officers controlling and managing the same, shall be audited by the proper authorities of the state. The amount so audited shall be a permanent funded debt against the state in favor of the fund sustaining the loss upon which not less than six per centum of annual interest shall be paid. The amount of indebtedness so created shall not be counted as a part of the indebtedness mentioned in Article XIII, Sec. 2.

§ 14. The legislature shall provide by law for the protection of the school lands from trespass or unlawful appropriation, and for their defense against all unauthorized claims or efforts to divert them from the school fund.

§ 15. The legislature shall make such provisions by general taxation, and by authorizing the school corporations to levy such additional taxes, as with the income from the permanent school fund shall secure a thorough and efficient system of common schools throughout the state.

§ 16. No appropriation of lands, money or other property or credits to aid any sectarian school shall ever be made by the state, or any county or municipality within the state, nor shall the state or any county or municipality within the state accept any grant, conveyance, gift or bequest of lands, money or other property to be used for sectarian purposes, and no sectarian instruction shall be allowed in any school or institution aided or supported by the state.

§ 17. No teacher, State, county, township or district school officer shall be interested in the sale, proceeds or profits of any book, apparatus or furniture used or to be used in any school in this state, under such penalties as shall be provided by law.

Article IX

COUNTY AND TOWNSHIP ORGANIZATION

§ 1. The legislature shall provide by general law for organizing new counties, locating the county seats thereof and changing county lines; but no new county shall be organized so as to include an area of less than twenty-four congressional townships, as near as may be without dividing a township or fractional township, nor shall the boundaries of any organized county be changed so as to reduce the same to a less area than above specified. All changes in county boundaries in counties already organized, before taking effect, shall be submitted to the electors of the county or counties to be affected thereby, at the next general election thereafter and be adopted by a majority of the votes cast in each county at such election. Counties now organized shall remain as they are unless changed according to the above provisions.

§ 2. In counties already organized where the county seat has not been located by a majority vote, it shall be the duty of the county board to submit the location of the county seat to the electors of said county at a general election. The place receiving the majority of all votes cast at said election shall be the county seat of said county.

§ 3. Whenever a majority of the legal voters of any organized county shall petition the county board to change the location of the county seat which has once been located by a majority vote, specifying the place to which it is to be changed, said county board shall submit the same to the people of said county at the next general election, and if the proposition to change the county seat be ratified by two-thirds of the votes cast at said election, then the county seat shall be changed, otherwise not. A proposition to change the location of the county seat of any organized county shall not again be submitted before the expiration of four years.

§ 4. The legislature shall provide by general law for organizing the counties into townships, having due regard for congressional township lines and natural boundaries, and whenever the population is sufficient and the natural boundaries will permit, the civil townships shall be co-extensive with the congressional townships.

§ 5. In each organized county at the first general election held after the admission of the State of South Dakota into the Union, and every two years thereafter, there shall be elected a clerk of the court, sheriff, county auditor, register of deeds, treasurer, state's attorney, surveyor, coroner, and superintendent of schools, whose terms of office respectively shall be two years, and except the clerk of the court, no person shall be eligible for more than four years in succession to any of the above named offices.

§ 6. The legislature shall provide by general law for such county, township and district officers as may be deemed necessary, and shall prescribe the duties and compensation of all county, township and district officers.

§ 7. All county, township and district officers shall be electors in the county, township or district in which they are elected, provided that nothing in this section shall prevent the holding of school offices by any person, as provided in Section 9, Article VII.

Article X

Municipal Corporations

§ 1. The legislature shall provide by general laws for the organization and classification of municipal corporations. The number of such classes shall not exceed four, and the powers of each class shall be defined by general laws, so that no such corporations shall have any powers, or be subject to any restrictions other than those of all corporations of the same class. The legislature shall restrict the power of such corporations to levy taxes and assessments, borrow money and contract debts, so as to prevent the abuse of such power.

§ 2. Except as otherwise provided in this constitution, no tax or assessment shall be levied or collected, or debts contracted by municipal corporations, except in pursuance of law, for public purposes specified by law; nor shall money raised by taxation, loan or assessment for one purpose ever be diverted to any other.

§ 3. No street passenger railway or telegraph or telephone lines shall be constructed within the limits of any village, town or city without the consent of its local authorities.

REVENUE AND FINANCE

§ 1. The legislature shall provide for an annual tax sufficient to defray the estimated ordinary expenses of the state, for each year, not to exceed in any one year two mills on each dollar of the assessed valuation of all taxable property in the state, to be ascertained by the last assessment made for state and county purposes.

And whenever it shall appear that such ordinary expenses shall exceed the income of the state for such year, the legislature shall provide for levying a tax for the ensuing year, sufficient with other sources of income, to pay the deficiency of the preceding year, together with the estimated expenses of such ensuing year. And for the purpose of paying the public debt, the legislature shall provide for levying a tax annually, sufficient to pay the annual interest and the principal of such debt within ten years from the final passage of the law creating the debt, provided that the annual tax for the payment of the interest and principal of the public debt shall not exceed in any one year two mills on each dollar of the assessed valuation of all taxable property in the state as ascertained by the last assessment made for the state and county purposes.

§ 2. All taxes to be raised in this state shall be uniform on all real and personal property, according to its value in money, to be ascertained by such rules of appraisement and assessment as may be prescribed by the legislature by general law, so that every person and corporation shall pay a tax in proportion to the value of his, her or its property. And the legislature shall provide by general law for the assessing and levying of taxes on all corporation property as near as may be by the same methods as are provided for assessing and levying of taxes on individual property.

§ 3. The power to tax corporations and corporate property shall not be surrendered or suspended by any contract or grant to which the state shall be a party.

§ 4. The legislature shall provide for taxing all moneys, credits, investments in bonds, stocks, joint stock companies, or otherwise; and also for taxing the notes and bills discounted or purchased, moneys loaned and all other property, effects or dues of every description, of all banks and of all bankers, so that all property employed in banking shall always be subject to a taxation equal to that imposed on the property of individuals.

§ 5. The property of the United States and of the state, county, and municpal corporations, both real and personal, shall be exempt from taxation.

§ 6. The legislature shall, by general law, exempt from taxation, property used exclusively for agricultural and horticultural societies, for school, religious, cemetery and charitable purposes, and personal property to any amount not exceeding in value two hundred dollars, for each individual liable to taxation.

§ 7. All laws exempting property from taxation, other than that enumerated in Sections 5 and 6 of this article, shall be void.

§ 8. No tax shall be levied except in pursuance of a law, which shall distinctly state the object of the same, to which the tax only shall be applied.

§ 9. All taxes levied and collected for state purposes shall be paid into the state treasury. No indebtedness shall be incurred or money expended by the state, and no warrant shall be drawn upon the state treasurer except in pursuance of an appropriation for the specific purpose first made. The legislature shall provide by suitable enactment for carrying this section into effect.

§ 10. The legislature may vest the corporate authority of cities, towns and villages with power to make local improvements by special taxation of contiguous property or otherwise. For all corporate purposes, all municipal corporations may be vested with authority to assess and collect taxes; but such tax shall be uniform in respect to persons and property within the jurisdiction of the body levying the same.

§ 11. The making of profit, directly or indirectly, out of state, county, city, town or school district money, or using the same for any purpose not authorized by law, shall be deemed a felony and shall be punished as provided by law.

§ 12. An accurate statement of the receipts and expenditures of the public moneys shall be published annually in such manner as the legislature may provide.

Article XII

PUBLIC ACCOUNTS AND EXPENDITURES

§ 1. No money shall be paid out of the treasury except upon appropriation by law and on warrant drawn by the proper officer.

§ 2. The general appropriation bill shall embrace nothing but appropriations for ordinary expenses of the executive, legislative and judicial departments of the state, the current expenses of state institutions, interest on the public debt, and for common schools. All other appropriations shall be made by separate bills, each embracing but one object, and shall require a two-thirds vote of all the members of each branch of the legislature.

§ 3. The legislature shall never grant any extra compensation to any public officer, employe, agent or contractor after the services shall have been rendered or the contract entered into, nor authorize the payment of any claims or part thereof created against the state, under any agreement or contract made without express authority of law, and all such unauthorized agreements or contracts shall be null and void; nor shall the compensation of any public officer be increased or diminished during his term of office; *Provided, however*, that the legislature may make appropriations for expenditures incurred in suppressing or repelling invasion.

§ 4. An itemized statement of all receipts and expenditures of the public moneys shall be published annually in such manner as the legislature shall provide, and such statements shall be submitted to the legislature at the beginning of each regular session by the governor with his message.

Article XIII

PUBLIC INDEBTEDNESS

§ 1. Neither the state nor any county, township or municipality shall loan or give its credit or make donations to or in aid of any individual, association or corporation except for the necessary support of the poor, nor subscribe to or become the owner of the capital stock of any association or corporation, nor pay or become responsible for the debt or liability of any individual, association or corporation; *Provided*, that the state may assume or pay such debt or liability when incurred in time of war for the defense of the state. Nor shall the state engage in any work of internal improvement.

§ 2. For the purpose of defraying extraordinary expenses and making public improvements, or to meet casual deficits or failure in revenue, the state may contract debts never to exceed, with previous debts, in the aggregate $100,000, and no greater indebtedness shall be incurred except for the purpose of repelling invasion, suppressing insurrection, or defending the state or the United States in war, and provision shall be made by law for the payment of the interest annually, and the principal when due, by tax levied for the purpose, or from other sources of revenue; which law providing for the payment of such interest and principal by such tax or otherwise shall be irrepealable until such debt is paid; *Provided, however*, the State of South Dakota shall have the power to refund the territorial debt assumed by the State of South Dakota, by bonds of the State of South Dakota.

§ 3. That the indebtedness of the State of South Dakota, limited by Sec. 2 of this article shall be in addition to the debt of the Territory of Dakota assumed by and agreed to be paid by South Dakota.

§ 4. *The debt of any county, city, town, school district or other subdivision, shall never exceed five per centum upon the assessed value of the taxable property therein.

In estimating the amount of indebtedness which a municipality or subdivision may incur, the amount of indebtedness contracted prior to the adoption of this constitution shall be included.

§ 5. Any city, county, town, school district or any other subdivision incurring indebtedness shall, at or before the time of so doing, provide for the collection of an annual tax sufficient to pay the interest and also the principal thereof when due, and all laws or ordinances providing for the payment of the interest or principal of any debt shall be irrepealable until such debt be paid.

§ 6. In order that the payment of the debts and liabilities contracted or incurred by and in behalf of the Territory of Dakota may be justly and equitably provided for and made, and in pursuance of the requirements of an act of congress approved Feb. 22, 1889, entitled, "An Act to provide for the division of Dakota into two states and to enable the people of North Dakota, South Dakota, Montana and Washington to form constitutions and state governments and to be admitted into the Union on an equal footing with the original states, and to make donations of public lands to such states," the states of North Dakota and South Dakota, by proceedings of a joint commission, duly appointed under said act, the sessions whereof were held in Bismarck in said State of North Dakota, from July 16, 1889, to July 31, 1889, inclusive, have agreed to the following adjustment of the amounts of the debts and liabilities of the Territory of Dakota which shall be assumed and paid by each of the States of North Dakota and South Dakota respectively, towit:

---

* See amendments, 1896, 1902.

1. This agreement shall take effect and be in force from and after the admission into the Union, as one of the United States of America, of either the State of North Dakota or the State of South Dakota.

2. The words "State of North Dakota" wherever used in this agreement, shall be taken to mean the Territory of North Dakota, in case the State of South Dakota shall be admitted into the Union prior to the admission into the Union of the State of North Dakota; and the words "State of South Dakota" wherever used in this agreement, shall be taken to mean the Territory of South Dakota in case the State of North Dakota shall be admitted into the Union prior to the admission into the Union of the State of South Dakota.

3. The said State of North Dakota shall assume and pay all bonds issued by the Territory of Dakota to provide funds for the purchase, construction, repairs or maintenance of such public institutions, grounds or buildings as are located within the boundaries of North Dakota, and shall pay all warrants issued under and by virtue of that certain act of the legislative assembly of the Territory of Dakota, approved March 3, 1889, entitled, "An Act to provide for the refunding of outstanding warrants drawn on the capitol building fund."

4. The said State of South Dakota shall assume and pay all bonds issued by the Territory of Dakota to provide funds for the purchase, construction, repairs or maintenance of such public institutions, grounds or buildings as are located within the boundaries of South Dakota.

5. That is to say: The State of North Dakota shall assume and pay the following bonds and indebtedness, to-wit: Bonds issued on account of the hospital for insane at Jamestown, North Dakota, the face aggregate of which is two hundred and sixty-six thousand dollars; also, bonds issued on account of the North Dakota University at Grand Forks, North Dakota, the face aggregate of which is ninety-six thousand seven hundred dollars; also, bonds issued on account of the penitentiary at Bismarck, North Dakota, the face aggregate of which is ninety-three thousand six hundred dollars; also, refunding capitol building warrants dated April 1, 1889, eighty-three thousand five hundred and seven dollars and forty-six cents.

And the State of South Dakota shall assume and pay the following bonds and indebtedness, towit: Bonds issued on account of the Hospital for the Insane at Yankton, South Dakota, the face aggregate of which is two hundred and ten thousand dollars; also, bonds issued on account of the school for deaf mutes at Sioux Falls, South Dakota, the face aggregate of which is fifty-one thousand dollars; also, bonds issued on account of the university at Vermillion, South Dakota, the face aggregate of which is seventy-five thousand dollars; also, bonds issued on account of the penitentiary at Sioux Falls, South Dakota, the face aggregate of which is ninety-four thousand three hundred dollars; also, bonds issued on account of agricultural college at Brookings, South Dakota, the face aggregate of which is ninety-seven thousand five hundred dollars, also, bonds issued on account of the normal school at Madison, South Dakota, the face aggregate of which is forty-nine thousand four hundred dollars; also, bonds issued on account of [the] school of mines at Rapid City, South Dakota, the face aggregate of which is thirty-three thousand dollars; also, bonds issued on account of the reform school at Plankinton, South Dakota, the face aggregate of which is thirty thousand dollars; also, bonds issued on account of the normal school at Spearfish, South Dakota, the face aggregate of which is twenty-five thousand dollars; also, bonds issued on account of the soldier's home at Hot Springs, South Dakota, the face aggregate of which is forty-five thousand dollars.

6. The states of North Dakota and South Dakota shall pay one-half each of all liabilities now existing or hereafter and prior to the taking effect of this agreement incurred, except those heretofore and hereafter incurred on account of public institutions, grounds or buildings, except as otherwise herein specifically provided.

7. The State of South Dakota shall pay to the State of North Dakota forty-six thousand five hundred dollars on account of the excess of territorial appropriations for the permanent improvement of territorial institutions which under this agreement will go to South Dakota, and in full of the undivided one-half interest of North Dakota in the territorial library, and in full settlement of unbalanced accounts, and of all claims against the territory of whatever nature, legal or equitable, arising out of the alleged erroneous or unlawful taxation of the Northern Pacific railroad lands, and the payment of said amount shall discharge and exempt the State of South Dakota from all liability for or on account of the several matters hereinbefore referred to; nor shall either state be called upon to pay or answer to any portion of liability hereafter arising or accruing on account of transactions heretofore had, which liability would be a liability of the territory of Dakota had such territory remained in existence, and which liability shall grow out of matters connected with any public institution, grounds or buildings of the territory situated or located within the boundaries of the other state.

8. A final adjustment of accounts shall be made upon the following basis: North Dakota shall be charged with all sums paid on account of the public institutions, grounds or buildings located within its boundaries on account of the current appropriations since March 8, 1889; and South Dakota shall be charged with all sums paid on account of public institutions, grounds or buildings located within its boundaries on the same account and during the same time. Each state shall be charged with one-half of all other expenses of the territorial government during the same time. All moneys paid into the treasury during the period from March 8, 1889, to the time of taking effect of this agreement by any county, municipality or person within the limits of the proposed State of North Dakota, shall be credited to the State of North Dakota; and all sums paid into said treasury within the same time by any county, municipality or person within the limits of the proposed State of South Dakota shall be credited to the State of South Dakota; except that any and all taxes on gross earnings paid into said treasury by railroad corporations since the eighth day of March, 1889, based upon earnings of years prior to 1888, under and by virtue of the act of the legislative assembly of the Territory of Dakota, approved March 7, 1889, and entitled "An Act providing for the levy and collection of taxes upon property of railroad companies in this territory," being Chapter 107 of the Session Laws of 1889, (that is, the part of such sum going to the territory) shall be equally divided between the States of North Dakota and South Dakota, and all taxes heretofore or hereafter paid into the said treasury under and by virtue of the act last mentioned, based on the gross

earnings of the year 1888, shall be distributed as already provided by law, except that so much thereof as goes to the territorial treasury shall be divided as follows: North Dakota shall have so [much] thereof as shall be or has been paid by railroads within the limits of the proposed State of North Dakota and South Dakota so much thereof as shall be or has been paid by railroads within the limits of the proposed State of South Dakota. Each state shall be credited also with all balances of appropriations made by the seventeenth legislative assembly of the Territory of Dakota for the account of public institutions, grounds or buildings situated within its limits, remaining unexpended on March 8, 1889. If there be any indebtedness except the indebtedness represented by the bonds and refunding warrants hereinbefore mentioned, each state shall at the time of such final adjustments of accounts, assume its share of said indebtedness as determined by the amount paid on account of the public institutions, grounds or buildings of such state in excess of the receipts from counties, municipalities, railroad corporations or persons within the limits of said state as provided in this article; and if there should be a surplus at the time of such final adjustment, each state shall be entitled to the amounts received from counties, municipalities, railroad corporations or persons within its limits over and above the amount charged to it.

§ 7. And the State of South Dakota hereby obligates itself to pay such part of the debts and liabilities of the Territory of Dakota as is declared by the foregoing agreement to be its proportion thereof, the same as if such proportion had been originally created by said State of South Dakota as its own debt or liability.

§ 8. The territorial treasurer is hereby authorized and empowered to issue refunding bonds to the amount of $107,000, bearing interest not to exceed the rate of four per cent per annum, for the purpose of refunding the following described indebtedness of the Territory of Dakota, towit:

Seventy-seven thousand five hundred dollars 5 per cent bonds, dated May 1, 1883, issued for the construction of the west wing of the insane hospital at Yankton, and $30,000 6 per cent bonds, dated May 1, 1883, issued for permanent improvements [of the] Dakota penitentiary at Sioux Falls, such refunding bonds, if issued, to run for not more than twenty years, and shall be executed by the governor and treasurer of the territory, and shall be attested by the secretary under the great seal of the territory.

In case such bonds are issued by the territorial treasurer as hereinbefore set forth, before the first day of October, 1889, then upon the admission of South Dakota as a state it shall assume and pay said bonds in lieu of the aforesaid territorial indebtedness.

Article XIV

STATE INSTITUTIONS

§ 1. The charitable and penal institutions of the State of South Dakota shall consist of a penitentiary, insane hospital, a school for the deaf and dumb, a school for the blind and a reform school.

§ 2. The state institutions provided for in the preceding section shall be under the control of a state board of charities and corrections, under such rules and restrictions as the legislature shall provide; such board to consist of not to exceed five members, to be appointed by the governor and confirmed by the senate, and whose compensation shall be fixed by law.

* § 3. The state university, the agricultural college, the normal schools and all other educational institutions that may be sustained either wholly or in part by the state shall be under the control of a board of nine members, appointed by the governor and confirmed by the senate, to be designated the regents of education. They shall hold their office for six years, three retiring every second year.

The regents in connection with the faculty of each institution shall fix the course of study in the same.

The compensation of the regents shall be fixed by the legislature.

§ 4. The regents shall appoint a board of five members for each institution under their control, to be designated the board of trustees. They shall hold office for five years, one member retiring annually. The trustees of each institution shall appoint the faculty of the same, and shall provide for the current management of the institution, but all appointments and removals must have the approval of the regents to be valid. The trustees of the several institutions shall receive no compensation for their services, but they shall be reimbursed for all expenses incurred in the discharge of their duties, upon presenting an itemized account of the same to the proper officer. Each board or trustees at its first meeting shall decide by lot the order in which its members shall retire from office.

§ 5. The legislature shall provide that the science of mining and metallurgy be taught in at least one institution of learning under the patronage of the state.

Article XV

MILITIA

§ 1. The militia of the State of South Dakota shall consist of all able-bodied male persons residing in the state, between the ages of eighteen and forty-five years, except such persons as now are, or hereafter may be, exempted by the laws of the United States or of this state.

§ 2. The legislature shall provide by law for the enrollment, uniforming, equipment and discipline of the militia, and the establishment of volunteer and such other organizations or both, as may be deemed necessary for the protection of the state, the preservation of order and the efficiency and good of the service.

§ 3. The legislature in providing for the organization of the militia shall conform, as nearly as practicable, to the regulations for the government of the armies of the United States.

§ 4. All militia officers shall be commissioned by the governor and may hold their commissions for such period of time as the legislature may provide, subject to removal by the governor for cause, to be first ascertained by a court-martial pursuant to law.

§ 5. The militia shall in [all] cases except treason, felony or breach of the peace be privileged from arrest during their attendance at muster and elections and in going to and returning from the same.

---

* See amendment, 1896.

§ 6. All military records, banners and relics of the state, except when in lawful use, shall be preserved in the office of the adjutant general as an enduring memorial of the patriotism and valor of South Dakota; and it shall be the duty of the legislature to provide by law for the safe keeping of the same.

§ 7. No person having conscientious scruples against bearing arms shall be compelled to do military duty in time of peace.

Article XVI

IMPEACHMENT AND REMOVAL FROM OFFICE

§ 1. The house of representatives shall have the sole power of impeachment.

The concurrence of a majority of all members elected shall be necessary to an impeachment.

§ 2. All impeachments shall be tried by the senate. When sitting for that purpose the senator shall be upon oath or affirmation to do justice acording to law and evidence. No person shall be convicted without the concurrence of two-thirds of the members elected. When the governor or lieutenant governor is on trial the presiding judge of the supreme court shall preside.

§ 3. The governor and other state and judicial officers except county judges, justices of the peace and police magistrates shall be liable to impeachment for drunkenness, crimes, corrupt conduct, or malfeasance or misdemeanor in office, but judgment in such cases shall not extend further than to removal from office and disqualification to hold any office of trust or profit under the state. The person accused whether convicted or acquitted, shall nevertheless be liable to indictment, trial, judgment and punishment according to law.

§ 4. All officers not liable to impeachment shall be subject to removal for misconduct or malfeasance or crime or misdemeanor in office or for drunkenness or gross incompetency, in such manner as may be provided by law.

§ 5. No officer shall exercise the duties of his office after he shall have been impeached and before his acquittal.

§ 6. On trial of an impeachment against the governor the lieutenant governor shall not act as a member of the court.

§ 7. No person shall be tried on impeachment before he shall have been served with a copy thereof at least twenty days previous to the day set for trial.

§ 8. No person shall be liable to impeachment twice for the same offense.

Article XVII

CORPORATIONS

§ 1. No corporation shall be created or have its charter extended, changed or amended by special laws except those for charitable, educational, penal or reformatory purposes, which are to be and remain under the patronage and control of the state; but the legislature shall provide by general laws for the organization of all corporations hereafter to be created.

§ 2. All existing charters, or grants of special or exclusive privileges, under which a *bona fide* organization shall not have taken place and business been commenced in good faith at the time this constitution takes effect, shall thereafter have no validity.

§ 3. The legislature shall not remit the forfeiture of the charter of any corporation now existing nor alter or amend the same nor pass any other general or special law for the benefit of such corporation, except upon the condition that such corporation shall thereafter hold its charter subject to the provisions of this constituion.

§ 4. The exercise of the right of eminent domain shall never be abridged or so construed as to prevent the legislature from taking the property and franchises of incorporated companies and subjecting them to public use, the same as the property of individuals, and the exercise of the police power of the state shall never be abridged or so construed as to permit corporations to conduct their business in such manner as to infringe the equal rights of individuals or the general well being of the state.

§ 5. In all elections for directors or managers of a corporation each member or shareholder may cast the whole number of his votes for one candidate, or distribute them upon two or more candidates as he may prefer.

§ 6. No foreign corporation shall do any business in this state without having one or more known places of business and an authorized agent or agents in the same upon whom process may be served.

§ 7. No corporation shall engage in any business other than that expressly authorized in its charter, nor shall it take or hold any real estate except such as may be necessary and proper for its legitimate business.

§ 8. No corporation shall issue stocks or bonds except for money, labor done, or money or property actually received; and all fictitious increase of stock or indebtedness shall be void. The stock and indebtedness of corporations shall not be increased except in pursuance of general law nor without the consent of the persons holding the larger amount in value of the stock first obtained, at a meeting to be held after sixty days' notice given in pursuance of law.

§ 9. The legislature shall have the power to alter, revise or annul any charter of any corporation now existing and revokable at the taking effect of this constitution, or any that may be created, whenever in their opinion it may be injurious to the citizens of this state, in such a manner, however, that no injustice shall be done to the incorporators. No law hereafter enacted shall create, renew or extend the charter of more than one corporation.

§ 10. No law shall be passed by the legislature granting the right to construct and operate a street railroad within any city, town or incorporated village without requiring the consent of the local authorities having the control of the street or highway proposed to be occupied by said such street railroad.

§ 11. Any association or corporation organized for the purpose, or any individual, shall have the right to construct and maintain lines of telegraph in this state, and to connect the same with other lines; and the legislature shall by general law of uniform operation provide reasonable regulations to give full effect to this section. No telegraph company shall consolidate with or hold a controlling interest in the stock or bonds of any other telegraph company owning a competing line or acquire by purchase or otherwise any other competing line of telegraph.

§ 12. Every railroad corporation organized or doing business in this state under the laws or authority thereof shall have and maintain a public office or place in this state for the transaction of its business, where transfers of its stocks shall be made and in which shall be kept for public inspection books in which shall be recorded the amount of capital stock subscribed, and by whom; the names of the owners of its stock, and the amount owned by them respectively; the amount of stock paid in, and by whom; the transfers of said stock; the amount of its assets and liabilities, and the names and place of residence of its officers. The directors of every railroad corporation shall annually make a report, under oath, to the auditor of public accounts or some officer or officers to be designated by law, of all their acts and doings, which report shall include such matters relating to railroads as may be prescribed by law, and the legislature shall pass laws enforcing by suitable penalties the provisions of this section.

§ 13. The rolling stock and all other movable property belonging to any railroad company or corporation in this state shall be considered personal property, and shall be liable to execution and sale in the same manner as the personal property of individuals, and the legislature shall pass no laws exempting such property from execution and sale.

§ 14. No railroad corporation shall consolidate its stock, property or franchises with any other railroad corporation owning a parallel or competing line; and in no case shall any consolidation take place except upon public notice given out, at least sixty days to all stockholders in such manner as may be provided by law. Any attempt to evade the provisions of this section, by any railroad corporation, by lease or otherwise, shall work a forfeiture of its charter.

§ 15. Railways heretofore constructed or that may hereafter be constructed, in this state, are hereby declared public highways, and all railroads and transportation companies are declared to be common carriers and subject to legislative control; and the legislature shall have power to enact laws regulating and controlling the rates of charges for the transportation of passengers and freight as such common carrier from one point to another in this state.

§ 16. Any association or corporation organized for the purpose shall have the right to construct and operate a railroad between any points within this state, and to connect at the state line with railroads of other states. Every railroad company shall have the right with its road to intersect, connect with, or cross any other railroad, and shall receive and transport each the other's passengers, tonnage and cars, loaded or empty, without delay or discrimination.

§ 17. The legislature shall pass laws to correct abuses and prevent discrimination and extortion in the rates of freight and passenger tariffs on the different railroads in this state, and enforce such laws by adequate penalties, to the extent, if necessary for that purpose, of forfeiture of their property and franchises.

§ 18. Municipal and other corporations and individuals invested with the privilege of taking private property for public use shall make just compensation for property taken, injured or destroyed, by the construction or enlargement of their works, highways or improvements, which compensation shall be paid or secured before such taking, injury or destruction. The legislature is hereby prohibited from depriving any person of an appeal from any preliminary assessment of damages against any such corporation or individuals made by viewers or otherwise, and the amount of such damages in all cases of appeal shall, on the demand of either party, be determined by a jury as in other civil cases.

§ 19. The term "corporations" as used in this article shall be construed to include all joint stock companies or associations having any of the powers or privileges of corporations not possessed by individuals or partnerships.*

Article XVIII

BANKING AND CURRENCY

§ 1. If a general banking law shall be enacted it shall provide for the registry and countersigning by an officer of this State of all bills or paper credit designed to circulate as money, and require security to the full amount thereof, to be deposited with the state treasurer, in the approved securities of the state or of the United States, to be rated at ten per centum below their par value, and in case of their depreciation the deficiency shall be made good by depositing additional securities.

§ 2. Every bank, banking company or corporation shall be required to cease all banking operation within twenty years from the time of its organization, and promptly thereafter close its business, but shall have corporate capacity to sue or be sued until its business is fully closed, but the legislature may provide by general law for the reorganization of such banks.

§ 3. The shareholders or stockholders of any banking corporation shall be held individually responsible and liable for all contracts, debts and engagements of such corporation to the extent of the amount of their stock therein, at the par value thereof, in addition to the amount invested in such shares or stock; and such individual liabilities shall continue for one year after any transfer or sale of stock by any stockholder or stockholders.

Article XIX

CONGRESSIONAL AND LEGISLATIVE APPORTIONMENT

§ 1. Until otherwise provided by law, the members of the house of representatives of the United States, apportioned to this state, shall be elected by the state at large.

§ 2. Until otherwise provided by law, the senatorial and representative districts shall be formed, and the senators and representatives shall be apportioned, as follows:

SENATORIAL DISTRICTS

District No. 1 shall consist of the county of Union and be entitled to one senator.

District No. 2 shall consist of the county of Clay, and be entitled to one senator.

---

* For new section, 20, see amendment, 1896.

District No. 3 shall consist of the county of Yankton, and be entitled to one senator.

District No. 4 shall consist of the county of Bon Homme, and be entitled to one senator.

District No. 5 shall consist of the county of Lincoln, and be entitled to one senator.

District No. 6 shall consist of the county of Turner, and be entitled to one senator.

District No. 7 shall consist of the county of Hutchinson, and be entitled to one senator.

District No. 8 shall consist of the counties of Charles Mix and Douglas, and be entitled to one senator.

District No. 9 shall consist of the county of Minnehaha, and be entitled to two senators.

District No. 10 shall consist of the county of McCook, and be entitled to one senator.

District No. 11 shall consist of the county of Hanson, and be entitled to one senator.

District No. 12 shall consist of the county of Davison, and be entitled to one senator.

District No. 13 shall consist of the county of Aurora, and be entitled to one senator.

District No. 14 shall consist of the county of Brule, and be entitled to one senator.

District No. 15 shall consist of the county of Moody, and be entitled to one senator.

District No. 16 shall consist of the county of Lake, and be entitled to one senator.

District No. 17 shall consist of the county of Miner, and be entitled to one senator.

District No. 18 shall consist of the county of Sanborn, and be entitled to one senator.

District No. 19 shall consist of the counties of Jerauld and Buffalo, and be entitled to one senator.

District No. 20 shall consist of the county of Brookings, and be entitled to one senator.

District No. 21 shall consist of the county of Kingsbury, and be entitled to one senator.

District No. 22 shall consist of the county of Beadle, and be entitled to one senator.

District No. 23 shall consist of the county of Hand, and be entitled to one senator.

District No. 24 shall consist of the counties of Hughes and Stanley, and be entitled to one senator.

District No. 25 shall consist of the counties of Sully and Hyde, and be entitled to one senator.

District No. 26 shall consist of the county of Deuel, and be entitled to one senator.

District No. 27 shall consist of the county of Hamlin, and be entitled to one senator.

District No. 28 shall consist of the county of Codington, and be entitled to one senator.

District No. 29 shall consist of the county of Clark, and be entitled to one senator.

District No. 30 shall consist of the county of Spink, and be entitled to one senator.

District No. 31 shall consist of the county of Grant, and be entitled to one senator.

District No. 32 shall consist of the county of Day, and be entitled to one senator.

District No. 33 shall consist of the county of Brown, and be entitled to two senators.

District No. 34 shall consist of the counties of Marshall and Roberts, and be entitled to one senator.

District No. 35 shall consist of the counties of Faulk and Potter, and be entitled to one senator.

District No. 36 shall consist of the counties of Edmunds and Walworth, and be entitled to one senator.

District No. 37 shall consist of the counties of McPherson and Campbell, and be entitled to one senator.

District No. 38 shall consist of the county of Lawrence, and be entitled to one senator.

District No. 39 shall consist of the county of Pennington, and be entitled to one senator.

District No. 40 shall consist of the counties of Meade and Butte, and be entitled to one senator.

District No. 41 shall consist of the counties of Custer and Fall River, and be entitled to one Senator.

REPRESENTATIVE DISTRICTS

District No. 1 shall consist of the county of Union, and be entitled to two representatives.

District No. 2 shall consist of the county of Clay, and be entitled to two representatives.

District No. 3 shall consist of the county of Yankton, and be entitled to three representatives.

District No. 4 shall consist of the county of Lincoln and be entitled to two representatives.

District No. 5 shall consist of the county of Turner, and be entitled to three representatives.

District No. 6 shall consist of the county of Hutchinson, and be entitled to three representatives.

District No. 7 shall consist of the county of Bon Homme, and be entitled to two representatives.

District No. 8 shall consist of the county of Douglas, and be entitled to one representative.

District No. 9 shall consist of the county of Charles Mix, and be entitled to one representative.

District No. 10 shall consist of the county of Minnehaha, and be entitled to five representatives.

District No. 11 shall consist of the county of McCook, and be entitled to two representatives.

District No. 12 shall consist of the county of Hanson, and be entitled to one representative.

District No. 13 shall consist of the county of Davison, and be entitled to one representative.

District No. 14 shall consist of the county of Sanborn, and be entitled to one representative.
District No. 15 shall consist of the county of Aurora, and be entitled to one representative.
District No. 16 shall consist of the counties of Jerauld and Buffalo, and be entitled to one representative.
District No. 17 shall consist of the county of Lake, and be entitled to three representatives.
District No. 18 shall consist of the county of Miner, and be entitled to two representatives.
District No. 19 shall consist of the county of Sanborn, and be entitled to two representatives.
District No. 20 shall consist of the county of Jerauld, and be entitled to one representative.
District No. 21 shall consist of the county of Buffalo, and be entitled to one representative.
District No. 22 shall consist of the county of Brookings, and be entitled to three representatives.
District No. 23 shall consist of the county of Kingsbury, and be entitled to three representatives.
District No. 24 shall consist of the county of Beadle, and be entitled to five representatives.
District No. 25 shall consist of the county of Hand, and be entitled to three representatives.
District No. 26 shall consist of the county of Hyde, and be entitled to one representative.
District No. 27 shall consist of the county of Hughes, and be entitled to one representative.
District No. 28 shall consist of the county of Sully, and be entitled to one representative.
District No. 29 shall consist of the county of Deuel, and be entitled to two representatives.
District No. 30 shall consist of the county of Hamlin, and be entitled to two representatives.
District No. 31 shall consist of the county of Codington, and be entitled to three representatives.
District No. 32 shall consist of the county of Clark, and be entitled to three representatives.
District No. 33 shall consist of the county of Spink, and be entitled to five representatives.
District No. 34 shall consist of the county of Faulk, and be entitled to two representatives.
District No. 35 shall consist of the county of Potter, and be entitled to one representative.
District No. 36 shall consist of the county of Grant, and be entitled to two representatives.
District No. 37 shall consist of the county of Roberts, and be entitled to one representative.
District No. 38 shall consist of the county of Day, and be entitled to three representatives.
District No. 39 shall consist of the county of Marshall and be entitled to two representatives.
District No. 40 shall consist of the county of Brown, and be entitled to eight representatives.

District No. 41 shall consist of the county of Potter, and be entitled to one representative.
District No. 42 shall consist of the county of Faulk, and be entitled to one representative.
District No. 43 shall consist of the county of Custer, and be entitled to one representative.
District No. 44 shall consist of the county of Fall River, and be entitled to one representative.
District No. 45 shall consist of the county of Pennington, and be entitled to two representatives.
District No. 46 shall consist of the county of Meade, and be entitled to one representative.
District No. 47 shall consist of the county of Butte, and be entitled to one representative.
District No. 48 shall consist of the county of Lawrence, and be entitled to three representatives.

Article XX

SEAT OF GOVERNMENT

§ 1. The question of the location of the temporary seat of government shall be submitted to a vote of the electors of the proposed State of South Dakota, in the same manner and at the same election at which this constitution shall be submitted, and the place receiving the highest number of votes shall be the temporary seat of government until a permanent seat of government shall be established as hereinafter provided.

§ 2. The legislature, at its first session after the admission of this state, shall provide for the submission of the question of a place for a permanent seat of government to the qualified voters of the state at the next general election thereafter, and that place which receives a majority of all the votes cast upon that question shall be the permanent seat of government.

§ 3. Should no place voted for at said election have a majority of all votes cast upon this question, the governor shall issue his proclamation for an election to be held in the same manner at the next general election to choose between the two places having received the highest number of votes cast at the first election on this question. This election shall be conducted in the same manner as the first election for the permanent seat of government, and the place receiving a majority of all the votes cast upon this question shall be the permanent seat of government.

Article XXI

MISCELLANEOUS

§ 1. *Seal and coat of arms.*] The design of the great seal of South Dakota shall be as follows: A circle within which shall appear in the left foreground a smelting furnace and other features of mining work. In the left background a range of hills. In the right foreground a farmer at his plow. In the right background a herd of cattle and a field of corn. Between the two parts thus described shall appear a river bearing a steamboat. Properly divided between the upper and lower edges of the circle shall appear the legend

"Under God the People Rule," which shall be the motto of the State of South Dakota. Exterior to this circle and within a circumscribed circle shall appear, in the upper part, the words " State of South Dakota." In the lower part the words " Great Seal," and the date in Arabic numerals of the year in which the state shall be admitted to the Union.

COMPENSATION OF PUBLIC OFFICERS

§ 2. The governor shall receive an annual salary of two thousand five hundred dollars; the judges of the supreme court shall each receive an annual salary of two thousand five hundred dollars; the judges of the circuit courts shall each receive an annual salary of two thousand dollars; *Provided*, that the legislature may, after the year one thousand eight hundred and ninety, increase the annual salary of the governor and each of the judges of the supreme court to three thousand dollars, and the annual salary of each of the circuit court judges to two thousand five hundred dollars.

The secretary of state, state treasurer and state auditor shall each receive an annual salary of one thousand eight hundred dollars; the commissioner of school and public lands shall receive an annual salary of one thousand eight hundred dollars; the superintendent of public instruction shall receive an annual salary of one thousand eight hundred dollars; the attorney general shall receive an annual salary of one thousand dollars; the compensation of the lieutenant governor shall be double the compensation of a state senator.

They shall receive no fees or perquisites whatever for the performance of any duties connected with their offices. It shall not be competent for the legislature to increase the salaries of the officers named in this article except as herein provided.

§ 3. *Oath of office.* Every person elected or appointed to any office in this state, except such inferior offices as may be by law exempted, shall, before entering upon the duties thereof, take an oath or affirmation to support the constitution of the United States and of this state, and faithfully to discharge the duties of his office.

§ 4. *Exemptions.*] The right of the debtor to enjoy the comforts and necessaries of life shall be recognized by wholesome laws; exempting from forced sale a homestead, the value of which shall be limited and defined by law, to all heads of families, and a reasonable amount of personal property, the kind and value of which to be fixed by general law.

§ 5. *Rights of married women.*] The real and personal property of any women in this state acquired before marriage, and all property to which she may after marriage become in any manner rightfully entitled, shall be her separate property, and shall not be liable for the debts of her husband.

Article XXII

COMPACT WITH THE UNITED STATES

The following articles shall be irrevocable without the consent of the United States and the people of the State of South Dakota expressed by their legislative assembly:

First—That perfect toleration of religious sentiment shall be secured, and that no inhabitant of this state shall ever be molested in person or property on account of his or her mode of religious worship.

Second—That we, the people inhabiting the State of South Dakota, do agree and declare that we forever disclaim all right and title to the unappropriated public lands lying within the boundary of South Dakota, and to all lands lying within said limits owned or held by any Indian or Indian tribes; and that until the title thereto shall have been extinguished by the United States, the same shall be and remain subject to the disposition of the United States; and said Indian lands shall remain under the absolute jurisdiction and control of the Congress of the United States; that the lands belonging to citizens of the United States residing without the said state shall never be taxed at a higher rate than the lands belonging to residents of this state; that no taxes shall be imposed by the State of South Dakota on lands or property therein belonging to or which may hereafter be purchased by the United States, or reserved for its use. But nothing herein shall preclude the State of South Dakota from taxing as other lands are taxed any lands owned or held by any Indian who has severed his tribal relation and has obtained from the United States, or from any person, a title thereto by patent or other grant, save and except such lands as have been or may be granted to any Indian or Indians under any act of Congress containing a provision exempting the lands thus granted from taxation. All such lands which may have been exempted by any grant or law of the United States shall remain exempt to the extent and as prescribed by such act of Congress.

Third—That the State of South Dakota shall assume and pay that portion of the debts and liabilities of the Territory of Dakota as provided by this constitution.

Fourth—That provision shall be made for the establishment and maintenance of systems of public schools, which shall be opened to all the children of this state, and free from sectarian control.

Article XXIII

AMENDMENTS AND REVISIONS OF THE CONSTITUTION

§ 1. Any amendment or amendments to this constitution may be proposed in either house of the legislature, and if the same shall be agreed to by a majority of the members elected to each of the two houses, such proposed amendment or amendments shall be entered on their journals, with the yeas and nays taken thereon, and it shall be the duty of the legislature to submit such proposed amendment or amendments to the vote of the people at the next general election. And if the people shall approve and ratify such amendment or amendments by a majority of the electors voting thereon, such amendment or amendments shall become a part of this constitution; *Provided*, that the amendment or amendments so proposed shall be published for a period of twelve weeks previous to the date of said election, in such manner as the legislature may provide; and *Provided further*, that if more than one amendment be submitted, they shall be submitted in such manner that the people may vote for or against such amendment separately.

§ 2. Whenever two-thirds of the members elected to each branch of the legislature shall think it necessary to call a convention to revise this constitution they shall recommend to the electors to vote at the next election for members of the legislature, for or against a convention; and if a majority of all the electors voting at said election shall have voted for a convention, the legislature shall, at their next session, provide by law for calling the same. The convention shall consist of as many members as the house of representatives of the legislature, and shall be chosen in the same manner, and shall meet within three months after their election for the purpose aforesaid.

Article XXIV

PROHIBITION

[To be submitted to a separate vote as provided by the schedule and ordinance.]

No person or corporation shall manufacture, or aid in the manufacture for sale, any intoxicating liquor; no person shall sell or keep for sale, as a beverage any intoxicating liquor. The legislature shall by law prescribe regulations for the enforcement of the provisions of this section and provide suitable and adequate penalties for the violation thereof. [Adopted October 1, 1889, by the following vote: For prohibition, 40,234; against prohibition, 34,510.]

Article XXV

MINORITY REPRESENTATION

[To be submitted to a separate vote as provided by the schedule and ordinance.]

§ 1. The house of representatives shall consist of three times the number of the members of the senate, and the term of office shall be two years. Three representatives shall be elected in each senatorial district at the first general election held after this constitution takes effect, and every two years thereafter.

§ 2. In all elections of representatives aforesaid each qualified voter may cast as many votes for one candidate as there are representatives to be elected, or may distribute the same, or equal parts thereof, among the candidates as he may see fit; and the candidates highest in votes shall be declared elected. [Rejected October 1, 1889, by the following vote: For minority representation, 24,161; against minority representation, 46,200.]

Article XXVI

SCHEDULE AND ORDINANCE

§ 1. That no inconvenience may arise from the change of the territorial government to the permanent state government it is hereby declared that all writs, actions, prosecutions, claims and rights of individuals, and all bodies corporate, shall continue as if no change had taken place in this government; and all process which may be before the organization of the judicial department under this constitution issued under the authority of the Territory of Dakota, within the boundary of this state, shall be as valid as if issued in the name of the State of South Dakota.

§ 2. That all fines, penalties, forfeitures and escheats accruing to the Territory of Dakota, within the boundary of the State of South Dakota, shall accrue to the use of said state.

§ 3. That all recognizances, bonds, obligations or other undertakings, heretofore taken, or which may be taken before the organization of the judicial department under this constitution shall remain valid, and shall pass over to, and may be prosecuted in the name of the State of South Dakota; and all bonds, obligations or undertakings executed to this territory, within the boundaries of the State of South Dakota, or to any officer in his official capacity, shall pass over to the proper state authority, and to their successors in office, for the uses therein respectively expressed, and may be sued for and recovered accordingly.

All criminal prosecutions and penal actions, which have arisen, or which may arise before the organization of the judicial department under this constitution, and which shall then be pending, may be prosecuted to judgment and executed in the name of the state.

§ 4. All officers, civil and military, now holding their offices and appointments in this territory under the authority of the United States, or under the authority of the Territory of Dakota, shall continue to hold and exercise their respective offices and appointments until superseded under this constitution; *Provided*, that the provisions of the above sections shall be subject to the provisions of the act of congress providing for the admission of the State of South Dakota, approved by the president of the United States on February 22, 1889.

§ 5. This constitution shall be submitted for adoption or rejection to a vote of the electors qualified by the laws of this territory to vote at all elections, at the election to be held on Tuesday, Oct. 1, 1889.

At the said election the ballots shall be in the following form:

For the constitution: Yes. No.
For prohibition: Yes. No.
For minority representation: Yes. No.

As a heading to each of said ballots shall be printed on each ballot the following instructions to voters:

All persons desiring to vote for the constitution, or for any of the articles submitted to a separate vote, must erase the word "No."

All persons who desire to vote against the constitution, or against any article submitted separately, must erase the word "Yes."

Any person may have printed or written on his ballot only the words "For the Constitution," or "Against the Constitution," and such ballots shall be counted for, or against the constitution accordingly. The same provision shall apply to articles submitted separately.

In addition to the foregoing election for the constitution and for the article submitted by this convention for a separate vote thereon, an election shall be held at the same time and places, by the said qualified electors, for the following state officers, to be voted for on the same ballot as above provided for votes on the constitution and separate articles, towit:

A governor, lieutenant governor, secretary of state, auditor, treasurer, attorney general, superintendent of public instruction, commissioner of school and public lands, judges of the supreme, circuit and county courts, representatives in congress, state senators, and representatives in the legislature.

All the elections above provided for shall be held in the same manner and form as provided for the election for the adoption or rejection of the constitution. And the names of all the officers above specified to be voted for at such election shall be written or printed upon the same ballots as the vote for or against the constitution.

The judges of election in counting the ballots voted at such election shall count all the affirmative ballots upon the constitution as votes for the constitution; and they shall count all the negative ballots voted at said election upon the constitution as votes against the constitution; and ballots voted at said election upon which neither of said words "Yes" or "No" following the words "For the Constitution" are erased, shall not be counted upon such proposition. And they shall count all affirmative ballots so voted upon the article on prohibition, separately submitted, as votes for such article, and they shall count all negative ballots so voted upon such article, as votes against such article; and ballots upon which neither the words "Yes" or "No" following the words "For Prohibition" are erased, shall not be counted upon such proposition; and they shall count all the affirmative ballots so voted upon the article on minority representation, separately submitted, as votes for such article. And they shall count all negative ballots so voted upon such article as votes against such article; and ballots upon which neither of said words "Yes" or "No" following the words "For Minority Representation" are erased, shall not be counted upon such proposition.

If it shall appear in accordance with the returns hereinafter provided for, that a majority of the votes polled at such election, for and against the constitution, are for the constitution, then this constitution shall be the constitution of the State of South Dakota. If it shall appear, according to the returns hereinafter provided for, that a majority of all votes cast at said election for and against "Prohibition" are for prohibition, then said Article XXIV shall be and form a part of this constitution, and be in full force and effect as such from date of said election, but if a majority of said votes shall appear, according to said returns to be against prohibition, then Article XXIV shall be null and void and shall not be a part of this constitution. And if it appear, according to the returns hereinafter provided for, that a majority of all votes cast at said election for and against "Minority Representation" are for minority representation, then Article XXV shall be and form a part of said constitution, and be in full force and effect as such from the date of said election; but if a majority of said votes shall appear, according to said returns, to be against minority representation, then said Article XXV shall be null and void and shall not be a part of this constitution.

At such election the person voted for, for any one of the offices to be filled at such election, who shall receive the highest number of votes cast at said election, shall be declared elected to said office.

§ 6. At the same time and places of election there shall be held by said qualified electors an election for the place of the temporary seat of government.

On each ballot, and on the same ballot on which are the matters voted for or against, as hereinbefore provided, shall be written or printed the words " For Temporary Seat of Government," (Here insert the name of the city, town or place, to be voted for.)

And upon the canvass and return of the vote, made as hereinafter provided for, the name of the city, town or place, which shall have received the largest number of votes for said temporary seat of government, shall be declared by the governor, chief justice and secretary of the Territory of Dakota, or by any two of them, at the same time that they shall canvass the vote for or against the constitution, together with the whole number of votes cast for each city, town or place, and the officers above named, shall immediately after the result of said election shall have been ascertained, issue a proclamation directing the legislature elected at said election to assemble at said city, town or place so selected, on the day fixed by this schedule and ordinance.

§ 7. The election provided for herein shall be under the provisions of the constitution herewith submitted, and shall be conducted in all respects as elections are conducted under the general laws of the Territory of Dakota, except as herein provided. No mere technicalities or informalities in the manner or form of election, or neglect of any officer to perform his duty with regard thereto, shall be deemed to vitiate or avoid the same, it being the true intent and object of this ordinance to ascertain and give effect to the true will of the people of the State of South Dakota, as expressed by their votes at the polls.

§ 8. Immediately after the election herein provided for, the judges of election at each voting place shall make a true and complete count of all the votes duly cast at such election, and shall certify and return the result of the same, with the names of all the candidates and the number of votes cast for each candidate, and the number of votes cast for and against the constitution, and the number of votes cast for and against prohibition, and the number of votes cast for and against minority representation, and the number of votes cast for each city, town or place for the " temporary seat of government," to the county clerk, or auditor of the respective counties, together with one of the poll lists and election books used in said election.

§ 9. Within five days after said election the several boards of county canvassers provided by law for the canvassing of the results of the election, shall make and certify to the secretary of the Territory of Dakota the true and correct return of the total number of votes cast for the constitution, and against the constitution, of the number of votes cast for and against " prohibition," and the number of votes cast for and against minority representation," and the number of votes cast for each city, town or place as the " temporary seat of government," and of the number of votes cast for each person voted for at such election, except county officers and members of the legislature, and shall transmit the same to the secretary of the Territory of Dakota, by mail, and shall file with the county clerk or auditor of each of said counties a duplicate and certified copy of said return.

Said board of county canvassers shall issue certificates of election to the persons who shall have received the highest number of votes cast for the respective offices of judge of the county court and representatives in the legislature, and for state senator or senators.

§ 10. When two or more counties are connected in one senatorial or representative district, it shall be the duty of the clerks and auditors of the respective counties to attend at the office of the county clerk of the senior county in the date of organization within twenty days after the date of election, and they shall compare the votes given in the several counties comprising such senatorial and representative district and such clerks or auditors shall immediately make out a certificate of election to the person having the highest number of votes in such district for state senator or representative or both; which certificate shall be delivered to the person entitled thereto on his application to the clerk of the senior county of such district.

§ 11. The secretary of the territory shall receive all returns of election transmitted to him as above provided, and shall preserve the same, and after they have been canvassed as hereinafter provided, and after the admission of the State of South Dakota into the Union, he shall deliver said returns to the proper state officer of said State of South Dakota.

Within fifteen days after said election the secretary of the territory, with the governor and chief justice thereof, or any two of them, shall canvass such returns and certify the same to the president of the United States, as provided in the enabling act.

They shall also ascertain the total number of votes cast at such election for the constitution and against the constitution; the total number of votes cast for and against prohibition; and the total number of votes cast for and against minority representation; and the total number of votes cast for each city, town, or place as the "temporary seat of government;" and the total number of votes cast for each person voted for, for any office at said election, excepting county judges and members of the legislature, and shall declare the result of said election in conformity with such vote, and the governor of the territory shall thereupon issue a proclamation at once thereof.

They shall also make and transmit to the state legislature, immediately upon its organization, a list of all the state and judicial officers who shall thus be ascertained to be duly elected.

The various county and district canvassing boards shall make and transmit to the secretary of the territory the names of all persons declared by them to be elected members of the senate and house of representatives of the state of South Dakota; he shall make separate lists of the senators and representatives so elected, which lists shall constitute the rolls under which the senate and house of representatives shall be organized.

The governor of the territory shall make and issue certificates of election to the persons who are shown by the canvass to have received the highest number of votes for governor, lieutenant governor, secretary of state, auditor, treasurer, attorney-general, superintendent of public instruction, commissioner of schools and public lands, and judges of the supreme and circuit courts. Such certificates to be attested by the secretary of the territory.

§ 12. The apportionment made in this constitution shall govern the elections above provided for for members of the state legislature, until otherwise provided by law.

At the first election held under this ordinance for senators and representatives of the legislature, there shall be elected forty-five senators and one hundred and twenty-four representatives in the state legislature respectively.

§ 13. The legislature elected under the provisions of this ordinance and constitution shall assemble at the temporary seat of government on the third Tuesday in October, in the year A. D. 1889, at 12 o'clock noon, and on the first day of their assemblage the governor and other state officers shall take the oath of office in the presence of the legislature. The oath of office shall be administered to the members of the legislature and to the state officers by the chief justice of the territory, or by any other officer duly authorized by the laws of the territory of Dakota to administer oaths.

§ 14. Immediately after the organization of the legislature and taking the oath of office by the state officers, the legislature shall then and there proceed to the election of two senators of the United States for the State of South Dakota, in the mode and manner provided by the laws of congress for the election of United States senators. And the governor and the secretary of the State of South Dakota shall certify the election of the said senators and two representatives in congress, in the manner required by law.

§ 15. Immediately after the election of the United States senators as above provided for, said legislature shall adjourn to meet at the temporary seat of government on the first Tuesday after the first Monday of January, 1890, at 12 o'clock M.; *Provided, however*, that if the State of South Dakota has not been admitted by proclamation or otherwise at said date, then said legislature shall convene within ten days after the date of the admission of the state into the Union.

§ 16. Nothing in this constitution or schedule contained shall be construed to authorize the legislature to exercise any powers except such as are necessary to its first organization, and to elect United States senators, and to adjourn as above provided. Nor to authorize an officer of the executive, administrative or judiciary departments to exercise any duties of his office until the State of South Dakota shall have been regularly admitted into the Union, excepting such as may be authorized by the congress of the United States.

§ 17. The ordinances and schedules enacted by this convention shall be held to be valid for all the purposes thereof.

§ 18. That we, the people of the State of South Dakota, do ordain:

First—That perfect toleration of religious sentiment shall be secured, and that no inhabitant of this state shall ever be molested in person or property on account of his or her mode of religious worship.

Second—That we, the people inhabiting the State of South Dakota, do agree and declare that we forever disclaim all right and title to the unappropriated public lands lying within the boundaries of South Dakota; and to all lands lying within said limits owned or held by any Indian or Indian tribes, and that until the title thereto shall have been extinguished by the United States the same shall be and remain subject to the disposition of the United States, and said Indian lands shall remain under the absolute jurisdiction and control of the congress of the United States; that the lands belonging to citizens of the United States residing without the said state shall never be taxed at a higher rate than the lands belonging to residents of this state.

That no taxes shall be imposed by the State of South Dakota on lands or property therein belonging to or which may hereafter be purchased by the United States, or reserved for its use. But nothing herein shall preclude the State of South Dakota from taxing as other lands are taxed, any lands owned or held by any Indian who has severed his tribal relation and has obtained from the United States or from any person a title thereto by patent or other grant, save and except such lands as have been or may be granted to any Indian or Indians under any act of Congress containing a provision exempting the lands thus granted from taxation; all such lands which may have been exempted by any grant or law of the United States shall remain exempt to the extent and as prescribed by such act of Congress.

Third—That the State of South Dakota shall assume and pay that portion of the debts and liabilities of the Territory of Dakota as provided in this constitution.

Fourth—That provision shall be made for the establishment and maintenance of systems of public schools which shall be opened to all the children of this state and free from sectarian control.

Fifth—That jurisdiction is ceded to the United States over the military reservations of Fort Mead, Fort Randall and Fort Sully, heretofore declared by the president of the United States; *Provided*, legal process, civil and criminal, of this state shall extend over such reservations in all cases of which exclusive jurisdiction is not vested in the United States, or of crimes not committed within the limits of such reservations.

These ordinances shall be irrevocable without the consent of the United States, and also the people of the said State of South Dakota expressed by their legislative assembly.

§ 19. The tenure of all officers, whose election is provided for in this schedule on the first day of October, A. D. 1889, shall be as follows:

The governor, lieutenant governor, secretary of state, auditor, treasurer, attorney general, superintendent of public instruction, commissioner of school and public lands, judges of county courts, shall hold their respective offices until the first Tuesday after the first Monday in January, A. D. 1891, at twelve o'clock, M., and until their successors are elected and qualified.

The judges of the supreme court and circuit courts shall hold their offices until the first Tuesday after the first Monday in January, A. D. 1894, at twelve o'clock M., and until their successors are elected and qualified; subject to the provisions of Sec. 26 of Article V of the constitution.

The terms of office of the members of the legislature elected at the first election held under the provisions of this constitution shall expire on the first Tuesday after the first Monday in January, one thousand eight hundred and ninety-one (1891.)

§ 20. That the first general election under the provisions of this constitution shall be held on the first Tuesday after the first Monday in November, 1890, and every two years thereafter.

§ 21. The following form of ballot is adopted:

CONSTITUTIONAL TICKET.

INSTRUCTIONS TO VOTERS.

All persons desiring to vote for the constitution, or for any of the articles submitted to a separate vote, may erase the word " No."
All persons who desire to vote against the constitution, or any articles separately submitted may erase the word " Yes."
For the Constitution: Yes. No.
For Prohibition: Yes. No.
For Minority Representation: Yes. No.
For_____as the temporary seat of government.

For Governor.

For Lieutenant Governor.

For Secretary of State.

For Auditor.

For Treasurer.

For Attorney General.

For Superintendent of Public Instruction.

For Commissioner of School and Public Lands.

For Judges of the Supreme Court.

First District_____
Second District_____
Third District_____
For Judge of the Circuit Court_____Circuit.

For Representatives in Congress.

For State Senator.

For Representative in the Legislature.

For County Judge.
----

§ 22. This constitution shall be enrolled and after adoption and signing by the convention shall be delivered to Hon. A. J. Edgerton, the president of the constitutional convention, for safe keeping, and by him to be delivered to the secretary of state as soon as he assumes the duties of his office, and printed copies thereof shall be prefixed to the books containing the laws of the state, and all future editions thereof.

The president of this convention shall also supervise the making of the copy that must be sent to the president of the United States;

said copy is to be certified by the president and chief clerk of this convention.

§ 23. " The agreement made by the joint commission of the constitutional conventions of North and South Dakota concerning the records, books and archives of the Territory of Dakota is hereby ratified and confirmed, which agreement is in the words following: That is to say: "

The following books, records and archives of the Territory of Dakota shall be the property of North Dakota, towit:

All records, books and archives in the offices of the governor and secretary of the territory (except records of articles of incorporation of domestic corporations, returns of election of delegates to the constitutional convention of 1889, for South Dakota, returns of elections held under the so-called local option law in counties within the limits of South Dakota, bonds of notaries public appointed for counties within the limits of South Dakota, papers relating to the organization of counties situate within the limits of South Dakota, all of which records and archives are part of the records and archives of said secretary's office; excepting also census returns from counties situate within the limits of South Dakota and papers relating to requisitions issued upon the application of officers of counties situate within the limits of South Dakota, all of which are part of the records and archives of said governor's office.)

And the following records, books and archives shall also be the property of the State of North Dakota, towit:

Vouchers in the office or in the custody of the auditor of this territory relating to expenditures on account of public institutions, grounds or buildings situate within the limits of North Dakota; one warrant register in the office of the treasurer of this territory, being a record of warrants issued under and by virtue of chapter twenty-four of the laws enacted by the eighteenth legislative assembly of Dakota territory; all letters, receipts and vouchers in the same office now filed by counties and pertaining to counties within the limits of North Dakota; paid and canceled coupons in the same office representing interest on bonds which said State of North Dakota is to assume and pay; reports of gross earnings of the year 1888 in the same office, made by corporations operating lines of railroad situated wholly or mainly within the limits of North Dakota; records and papers of the office of the public examiner of the second district of the territory; records and papers of the office of the second district board of agriculture; records and papers in the office of the board of pharmacy of the district of North Dakota.

All records, books and archives of the Territory of Dakota which it is not herein agreed shall be the property of North Dakota, shall be the property of South Dakota.

The following books shall be copied and the copies shall be the property of North Dakota, and the cost of such copies shall be borne equally by the said states of North Dakota and South Dakota. That is to say:

Appropriation ledger for the years ending November, 1889 and 1890—one volume.

The current warrant auditor's register—one volume.

Insurance record for 1889—one volume.

Treasurer's cash book " D."

Assessment ledger " B."
Dakota Territory bond register—one volume.
Treasurer's current ledger—one volume.

The originals of the foregoing volumes which are to be copied, shall at any time after such copying shall have been completed, be delivered on demand to the proper authorities of the State of South Dakota.

All other records, books and archives which it is hereby agreed shall be the property of South Dakota shall remain at the capital of North Dakota until demanded by the legislature of the State of South Dakota, and until the State of North Dakota shall have had a reasonable time after such demand is made to provide copies or abstracts or such portions thereof as the said State of North Dakota may desire to have copies or abstracts of.

The State of South Dakota may also provide copies or abstracts of such records, books and archives which is agreed shall be the property of North Dakota as said State of South Dakota shall desire to have copies or abstracts of.

The expense of all copies or abstracts of records, books and archives which it is herein agreed may be made, shall be borne equally by said two states.*

ALONZO J. EDGERTON,
President of the Constitutional Convention.

Attest:
F. A. BURDICK, *Chief Clerk.*

AMENDMENTS

(November 8, 1898)[a]

ART. III. SEC. 1. The legislative power shall be vested in a legislature which shall consist of a Senate and House of Representatives. Except that the people expressly reserve to themselves the right to propose measures, which measures the legislature shall enact and submit to a vote of the electors of the state, and also the right to require that any laws which the legislature may have enacted shall be submitted to a vote of the electors of he state before going into effect (except such laws as may be necessary for the immediate preservation of the public peace, health or safety, support of state government and the existing public institutions.)

Provided, That not more than five per centum of the qualified electors of the state shall be required to invoke either the initiative or the referendum.

This section shall not be construed so as to deprive the legislature or any member thereof of the right to propose any measure. The veto power of the executive shall not be exercised as to measures referred to a vote of the people. This section shall apply to municipalities. The enacting clause of all laws approved by vote of the electors of the state shall be: " Be it enacted by the people of South Dakota." The legislature shall make suitable provisions for carrying into effect the provisions of this section.

---

* See amendment, 1900.

[a] This section was submitted in its present form by the legislature in 1897 as an amendment to the Constitution; (Chap. 39, Laws of 1897.) It was adopted by the people at the general election held November 8, 1898.

(November 4, 1902)

ART. VIII. SEC. 11. The rate of interest upon all investments of the permanent school or other educational funds mentioned in Sec. 11 of Art. VIII of the constitution of this state is hereby changed and reduced from six per centum per annum to five per centum per annum, wherever the said words " six per centum per annum " occur in said section. That if the foregoing amendment shall be approved and ratified by the people at said election, as provided by Article XXIII of the constitution, said Section 11 of Article VIII of the constitution shall be thereby amended by striking out the said words, " six per centum per annum " wherever they occur in said Section 11 and substituting in lieu thereof the words " five per centum per annum."

(November 8, 1904)

ART. VIII. SEC. 2. The moneys of the permanent school and other educational funds shall be invested only in first mortgages upon good improved farm lands within this state, as hereinafter provided or in bonds of school corporations within this state, or in bonds of the United States or of the State of South Dakota, or of any organized county, township or incorporated city in said state. The legislature shall provide by law the method of determining the amount of said funds, which shall be invested from time to time in such classes of securities respectively, taking care to secure continuous investments as far as possible.

All moneys of said funds which may from time to time be designated for investment in farm mortgages and in the bonds of school corporations, or in bonds or organized counties, townships or incorporated cities within this state, shall for such purpose be divided among the organized counties of the state in proportion to population as nearly as provisions by law to secure continuous investment may permit. The several counties shall hold and manage the same as trust funds, and they shall be and remain responsible and accountable for the principal and interest of all such moneys received by them from the date of receipt until returned because not loaned; and in case of loss of any money so apportioned to any county, such county shall make the same good out of its common revenue. Counties shall invest said money in bonds of school corporations, counties, townships or cities, or in first mortgages upon good improved farm lands within their limits respectively. The amount of each loan shall not exceed one-third of the actual value of the lands covered by the mortgage given to secure the same, such value to be determined by the board of county commissioners of the county in which the land is situated, and in no case shall more than five thousand dollars ($5,000) be loaned to any one person, firm or corporation, and the rate of interest shall not be less than five per cent per annum, and shall be such other and higher rate as the legislature may provide, and shall be payable semi-annually on the first day of January and July; Provided, that whenever there are moneys of said fund in any county amounting to one thousand dollars that cannot be loaned according to the provisions of this section, and any law pursuant thereto, the said sum may be returned to the state treasurer to be entrusted to some other county or counties, or otherwise invested under the provisions of this section.

Each county shall semi-annually, on the first day of January and July, render an account of the condition of the funds intrusted to it to the auditor of state, and at the same time pay to or account to the state treasurer for the interest due on all funds intrusted to it.

The legislature may provide by general law that counties may retain from interest collected in excess of five per centum per annum upon all said funds intrusted to them, not to exceed one per centum per annum. But no county shall be exempted from the obligation to make semi-annual payments to the state treasurer of interest at the rate provided by law for such loans, except only said one per centum, and in no case shall the interest, so to be paid, be less than five per centum per annum.

The legislature shall provide by law for the safe investment of the permanent school and other educational funds and for the prompt collection of interest and income thereof, and to carry out the objects and provisions of this section.

(1902)

[a]ART. IX. SEC. 3. Whenever a majority of the legal voters of any organized county shall petition the county board to change the location of the county seat which has once been located by a majority vote, specifying the place to which it is to be changed, said county board shall submit the same to the people of said county at the next general election, and if the proposition to change the county seat be ratified by two-thirds of the votes cast at said election, then the county seat shall be changed, otherwise not. A proposition to change the location of the county seat of any organized county shall not again be submitted before the expiration of four years.

(1896)

[b]ART. XIII. SEC. 4. The debt of any county, city, town, school district, civil township, or other subdivision, shall never exceed (5) five per centum upon the assessed value of the taxable property therein. In estimating the amount of indebtedness which a municipality or subdivision may incur the amount of indebtedness prior to the adoption of this constitution shall be included.

Provided, That any county, municipal corporation, civil township, district or other subdivision, may incur an additional indebtedness not exceeding ten per centum upon the assessed value of the taxable property therein for the purpose of providing water for irrigation and domestic uses: *Provided further*, That no county, municipal corporation or civil township shall be included within any such district or subdivision without a majority vote in favor thereof of the electors of the county, municipal corporation or civil township, as the case may be, which is proposed to be included therein, and no such debt

---

[a] Amended by popular vote of 36,436 for, to 14,612 against, at the general election held November 4, 1902.

[b] Submitted by the legislature in 1895, as an amendment to Section 4 of Article 13, of the Constitution, and was adopted at the general election of 1896 by a vote of 28,490 for, and 14,789 against.

That at the general election held on November 4, 1902, Section 4 of Article 13 of the Constitution was amended by a popular vote of 32,810 for to 13,599 against.

shall ever be incurred for any of the purposes in this section provided; unless authorized by a vote in favor thereof of a majority of the electors of such county, municipal corporation, civil township, district or subdivision incurring the same.

(November 4, 1902)

ART. XIII. SEC. 4. The debt of any county, city, town, school district, civil township or other subdivision, shall never exceed five (5) per centum upon the assessed valuation of the taxable property therein for the year preceding that in which said indebtedness is incurred.

In estimating the amount of the indebtedness which a municipality or subdivision may incur, the amount of indebtedness contracted prior to the adoption of this constitution shall be included.

Provided, That any county, municipal corporation, civil township, district or other subdivision may incur an additional indebtedness not exceeding ten per centum upon the assessed valuation of the taxable property therein for the year preceding that in which said indebtedness is incurred for the purpose of providing water and sewerage for irrigation, domestic uses, sewerage and other purposes; and

Provided, That in a city where the population is 8,000 or more, such city may incur an indebtedness not exceeding eight per centum upon the assessed valuation of the taxable property therein for the year next preceding that in which said indebtedness is incurred for the purpose of constructing street railways, electric lights or other lighting plants.

Provided further, That no county, municipal corporation, civil township, district or subdivision shall be included within such district or subdivision without a majority vote in favor thereof of the electors of the county, municipal corporation, civil township, district, or other subdivision as the case may be, which is purposed to be included therein, and no such debt shall ever be incurred for any of the purposes in this section provided, unless authorized by a vote in favor thereof by a majority of the electors of such county, municipal corporation, civil township, district or subdivision incurring the same.

(1896)

ART. XIV. SEC. 3.[a] The state university, the agricultural college, the normal schools and other educational institutions that may be sustained either wholly or in part by the state shall be under the control of a board of five members appointed by the governor and confirmed by the senate under such rules and restrictions as the legislature shall provide. The legislature may increase the number of members to nine.

ART. XIV. SEC. 4.[b] Stricken out, 1896, from original constitution.

[a] Submitted as an amendment to Constitution, Article 14, § 3, by the legislature in 1895, and at the general election in 1896, was adopted by the following vote: 31,061 for, and 11,690 against.
[b] Stricken from the Constitution, by an amendment submitted by the legislature in 1895, and adopted by the popular vote at the general election in 1896: 31,061 for, and 11,690 against.

(1896)

ART. XVII. SEC. 20.[a] Monopolies and trusts shall never be allowed in this state, and no incorporated company, co-partnership or association of persons in this state shall directly or indirectly combine or make any contract with any incorporated company, foreign or domestic, through their stockholders, or the trustees or assigns of such stockholders, or with any co-partnership or association of persons, or in any manner whatever to fix the prices, limit the production or regulate the transportation of any product or commodity so as to prevent competition in such prices, production or transportation, or to establish excessive prices therefor.

The legislature shall pass laws for the enforcement of this section by adequate penalties and in the case of incorporated companies, if necessary for that purpose, may, as a penalty, declare a forfeiture of their franchises.

ART. XXIV. (Prohibition) adopted, 1896.[b]
ART. XV. (Minority representation) rejected, 1889.[c]
ART. XXVI. Obsolete, except sections 17 and 18.[d]
ART. XXVII. (The control of, manufacture, and sale of liquor.)[e]

(1900)

ART. XXVIII.[f] SEC. 1. The several counties of the state shall invest the money of the permanent school and endowment funds in bonds of school, corporation, state, county and municipal bonds, or in first mortgages upon good improved farm lands within their limits respectively; under such regulations as the legislature may provide, but no farm loan shall exceed one thousand dollars to any one person or corporation.

---

[a] Submitted as an amendment to the Constitution, by the legislature in 1895, and was adopted by a popular vote of the electors of the state at the general election in 1896, by the following vote, for 36,763, against 9,136.

[b] Adopted at the time of the adoption of the Constitution, October 1st, 1889, it being voted upon separately, by the following vote: For, 40,234; against, 34,510. The legislature in 1895 submitted an amendment for the repeal of this article (24), which was adopted by a popular vote of the electors at the general election in 1896, by a vote of 31,901 for, and 24,910 against.

[c] Submitted to a separate vote, at the time of the adoption of the Constitution, October 1st, 1889, and was rejected by a vote of 24,161 for, and 46,200 against.

[d] As the provisions of this article (26), with the exception of Sections 17 and 18 thereof, have become obsolete, or fully executed, they have been omitted from this compilation.

[e] Article 27 of the constituion, providing that the manufacture and sale of liquor should be under exclusive state control, was submitted by the legislature in 1897, and adopted by a vote of the people at the general election in 1898, by a vote of 22,170 for, and 20,557 against. The legislature in 1899 submitted an amendment repealing Article 27, and at the general election held in 1900 the amendment was adopted by a vote of 48,673 for, and 33,927 against.

[f] Proposed by the legislature in 1899 as an amendment to the Constitution and was at the general election held in November, 1900, adopted by a popular vote of 49,989 for, and 15,653 against.

SELECTED DOCUMENTS

The documents selected for this section have been chosen to reflect the interests or attitudes of the contemporary observer or writer. Documents relating specifically to the constitutional development of South Dakota will be found in volume nine of <u>Sources and Documents of United States Constitutions</u>, a companion reference collection to the Columbia University volumes previously cited.

DOCUMENTS 93

FACTS ABOUT SOUTH DAKOTA - 1890'S

The following statements and
newspaper items present a
picture of many aspects of
life in the state.

Source: <u>More Facts About South Dakota Regarding Agriculture, Sheep Raising, Climate, Soil and Its Other Resources</u>. N.P., 1892, 10-39.

No More Pioneering.

There is now no free Government land in South Dakota east of the Missouri River, except in Faulk, Edmunds, Walworth, Campbell, McPherson and McIntosh counties (see map), where it still can be found in large tracts. The Government land office for that district is located at Aberdeen, S.D. West of the Missouri River in the Sioux Reservation there is also a great deal of free land still offered, which may be taken up under the pre-emption or homestead laws. Most of the state of South Dakota, especially the portion east of the Missouri River, is so well settled up now that the new comer is no longer a pioneer. The pioneering was done ten, twenty, or even thirty years ago. He finds himself with neighbors all around him. Schoolhouses and churches have been built. Railroads run through all localities. Towns have grown up everywhere. The farmer to-day gets good prices for his grain and stock, while he buys his supplies very nearly as cheaply as can be done anywhere. The man who now comes can get the benefit of cheap lands, without undergoing the hardships and inconveniences of pioneer life. Then, too, as many things must be done differently from the methods which prevail east, he can profit from the experience of his neighbors. In a word, the whole situation is changed since the first settlement of the country. Then everything was new, untried and uncertain. Now the farmer does not grope in the dark. Experiences has taught just what can be done and how best to do it. Barring the accidents and drouth and hail, which are incident to any country, the farmer knows that harvest will certainly follow seed time.

The Corn Belt of South Dakota.

While there is no sudden "jumping off" place where corn ceases to be safe and sure, the corn belt is generally made to include all of that section of the state for a distance of ninety miles northward from the Missouri River at Yankton; or say fifty miles north of the southern boundary of Minnesota extended. This area includes the counties of Union, Clay, Yankton, Bon Homme, Charles Mix, Douglas, Hutchinson, Turner, Lincoln, Minnehaha, McCook, Hanson, Davison, Aurora, Brule, Buffalo, Jerauld, Sanborn, Miner, Lake, Moody; also the corresponding section west of the Missouri and a large part of the Black Hills country. Of course, it is not meant that corn will not grow north of this section. As a matter of fact, excellent fields of corn have been grown in all parts of South Dakota; but there is more risk in the northern part of the state than in the southern part. In the bottom lands of the Missouri, seventy-five to one hundred bushels to the acre are not unusual yields; but as one goes northward, the yield is less and the danger from early frost is greater. The region included in the counties named is the oldest settled and the most prosperous part of the state. The farmers have raised excellent crops of wheat and other small grain; but after all, the wealth has been derived mostly from corn, hogs and cattle. Notwithstanding the fact that most of this section has been settled for twenty years and upward, that good crops have been grown every year — except the grasshopper period during the 'seventies, that there has never been any serious deficiency in the rainfall, that good water is always obtainable at a depth of from ten to twenty-five feet, that the climate is one of the most healthful in the world, that all necessary railroads have been built, that schools and churches abound, and that towns are numerous—notwithstanding all these facts, land is still cheap.

A Sample of What South Dakota Can Do.

The year 1891 justified the claims which have always been made for South Dakota. Those who by long residence have fully understood the resources of the state, have asserted that no section of the country could surpass South Dakota in general productiveness. Last year demonstrates the truthfulness of this claim in a way which can admit of no doubt. The claim has been proven many times before. All parts of South Dakota have produced big crops heretofore, but so little land was under cultivation that the good result was largely lost sight of. Then came the period of drouth, which lasted in a large part of the state for two years. This gave occasion for the cry of "destitution" and "hard times," which almost completely stopped immigration into the state. Yet, during this dry spell, the equal of which the old settler had never before experienced, the farmers of nearly all the state had fair, and, in some locations, first-class crops. The noteworthy thing about 1891 was, that while the rainfall was slightly below the average, yet the timeliness of the showers caused the grain to grow well, and fields yielded from eighteen to forty-two bushels of wheat per acre. To the farmer of the Northwest there is nothing strange in the fact that a field of wheat should yield forty bushels to the acre, for he has occasionally seen such things ever since he came into the country; but the gratifying thing about 1891 was that this large yield was, with few exceptions, characteristic of every county in the state. Taken as a whole, the farmers of South Dakota found themselves with, perhaps, the best crop they had ever known. Not only this, but, to make a good thing still better, the prices ranged higher than for several years. Wheat has sold for from seventy to eighty-five cents, according to time and locality, and these prices leave the farmer a handsome profit. What is true of wheat is likewise true of corn, oats, barley, and everything else the farmer had to sell.

In view of the low price at which land may be bought in South Dakota, in thousands of cases the value of last year's crop was more than sufficient to pay all the expense of growing a crop and to buy the land besides. In the East, a man is fortunate who can pay for his farm and improvements before old age overtakes him, and nowhere outside of the Northwest can a single crop pay for the land upon which it was grown.

Another good effect of that fine crop was that farmers who were compelled to run into debt for stock or improvements were able to take up their mortgages, and many have paid up their entire indebtedness and bought land besides. Others have been able to put up new houses and barns, while others have bought live stock for their farms. In all cases the farmers find themselves in better condition to face the future, and are firm in the belief that South Dakota is a good enough country to suit anybody.

What South Dakota Will Produce.

While here as elsewhere some things will grow better than others, it may be said there is no cereal, vegetable or flower grown in this latitude in the United States which will not grow in South Dakota. The vast majority of the people are engaged in farming and stock raising, and this must always be the occupation of most of those who make their home in this state. As agriculture is the basis of all wealth, South Dakota is destined always to be a prosperous if not a wealthy commonwealth. As yet only a small part of the land is under cultivation, but the time is not far distant when this state will feed a by no means insignificant portion of the world.

Healthfulness of the Climate.

There is, perhaps, nowhere on the continent a more healthful climate than that of South Dakota. The new comer does not have to get acclimated. The chills and fever, and malarial troubles generally, which used to be regarded as an unavoidable incident to the settlement of a new country, are practically unknown here. There is no low, swampy ground to breed malaria. The air is dry, pure and invigorating. The stranger from the East takes delight in inhaling the health-giving air of this section. He finds in it something which invigorates. He is told that it is ozone, and from henceforth, especially if he has weak lungs, he thanks God for ozone, even if he has but a vague idea of what ozone really is. This climate is especially grateful to those who have pulmonary troubles. Many persons have come here as a last resort and, instead o dying, have become robust and strong. The dyspeptic will be able to think of something else besides his stomach; the hollow-chested young fellow will develop an astonishing lung power; and those suffering from malaria will have the poison driven from their system. In general, the weak will be made strong, and the strong will increase their strength. The sick will be made well, and the well will develop into a vigorous physical condition. Of course, people must die here as elsewhere, but figures demonstrate that for good health and long life South Dakota beats the world.

Population.

The population of that part of the old territory of Dakota now known as

South Dakota, as nearly as can be ascertained, according to the census of 1880 was 98,268. The population returned under the present census for the state is 328,808. This shows an increase of 230,540, or 234.60 per cent.

The population of the ten cities having 2,000 or more inhabitants, in the order of their rank, is as follows:

CITIES.	COUNTIES.	POPULATION.		INCREASE.	
		1890.	1880.	Number.	Per cent.
Sioux Falls	Minnehaha	10,177	2,164	8,013	370.29
Yankton	Yankton	3,670	3,431	239	6.97
Pierre	Hughes	3,235			
Aberdeen	Brown	3,182			
Huron	Beadle	3,038	164	2,874	1,752.44
Watertown	Codington	2,672	746	1,926	258.18
Lead City	Lawrence	2,581	1,437	1,144	79.61
Deadwood	Lawrence	2,366	3,777	*1,411	*37.36
Mitchell	Davison	2,217	320	1,897	592.81
Rapid City	Pennington	2,128	292	1,836	628.77

* Decrease.

Educational Interests.

Aside from the state educational institutions, there are several excellent denominational colleges. The oldest and farthest advanced is Yankton College, established by the Congregationalists of South Dakota. The others are the Sioux Falls University, by the Baptists; Dakota University at Mitchell, and the Black Hills College at Hot Springs, by the Methodists; the Pierre University, by the Presbyterians; All Saints School for young ladies and children, by the Protestant Episcopalians, under Bishop Hare, and Norwegian Lutheran College at Canton. In a few years South Dakota will have a school fund which will be sufficient to meet all the expenses incident to the common school system of the state. Aside from special gifts to the different state institutions, the state inherited the sixteenth and thirty-sixth sections of every township. One-eighteenth of all land will amount to about 2,700,000 acres. If sold at the minimum price this land would bring $27,000,000. At six per cent. this will yield a fund of $1,600,000. The total expense of maintaining the common school system in 1890, including the city schools, was $1,439,531. This expense includes interest on bonds, redemption of bonds and other extraordinary expenses. Hence the total estimated income from the prospective school fund is nearly $200,000 in excess of the total school expenses of 1890. As expenses increase with the increase of the school population so will the school fund increase, since none of the land may be sold for less than $10, while much of it is selling for $20, and some will eventually bring as high as $50 and $100, and even more. A large acreage has been rented, and this rental will add a large sum to the school fund. Hence it will appear that before many years South Dakota will have an excellent system of common schools without any school tax.

Aurora County, South Dakota.

To-day, in Aurora county, near the thriving cities of Plankinton and White Lake, within sight and sound of the locomotive, lands can be purchased at a price less than the value of the first crop it will produce.

These lands are near to market, contiguous to town and elevators; estates of the richest soil under heaven, can be bought at one-tenth of the cost of a farm in the Eastern states. It is true these lands in Aurora county will one day be worth as much as land in any part of the Eastern states, but that time has not yet arrived, and, pending its arrival, fortunes may be made. A settler in Aurora county can have all the advantages of a high state of civilization—of railroad, churches, schools, society, and all the comforts and conveniences of the older portions of the state with the advantages of a new country combined therewith; you can plow and sow and reap on soil within the sound of the scream of the locomotive; you can raise crops from the strong, fertile, virgin soil, within a few hours of market; you can purchase deeded land in Aurora county to day from $4 to $10 per acre, and in many instances with some improvements. Parties who are renting worn out soil in the east cannot like being another man's servant, when such a golden opportunity is in their grasp. They can purchase lands at a price that the first year's crop will more than pay for, surrounded by more of the accessories that make life to the average man worth living, than can be found in the east that cost ten times as much. There is no fear that crops will be a failure, for there never has been a failure. The opportunities are even greater in the boundaries of Aurora county now than when the first white man crossed the Mississippi river, and the hardships that those who arrived to begin the construction of a great commonwealth suffered are now impossible. In settling in this country, you know that every train brings settlers that, becoming your neighbors, increase the selling price of your lands, so it is only a question of time when you can dispose of your property, if you desire, the increase of which will enable you to live in luxury and comfort.

The wealthy farmers of the states have not made their money by the crop the soil provided as much as by the increasing value of their lands. The man who purchases 160 acres of land in Aurora county for $6 per acre, according to improvements, will realize $20 per acre rise within ten years. The start made by a few brave and resolute spirits, who first settled the county, has swept on even to the present time, and the continuance of which has received no check since its inauguration. Acre after acre of the black mould has been turned upward towards the shining sun; house after house erected, and settler after settler has made himself a home to shelter himself and little ones from blasts that are more cruel than those of the winter. Each and every one of these settlers have prospered, and if a farm equal in area to the one they have here should be given them among the hills and stones of the east, they would refuse to give their Aurora county farm in exchange.

Where nature has done her part of the work as thoroughly as she has in Aurora county, there remains less for man to do, and there are classes of men who are bound to find out these choice places.

NEWSPAPER ITEMS.

Plankinton Standard: A. B. Johnson threshed a field of oats that turned out 60 bushels to the acre.

Farmers are about through with their harvest of small grain. No county eve. gathered in a richer grain harvest than our people this year. The farmers feel good, the merchants feel good, and only the railroad company is troubled—they don't know where to get cars to move the great amount of grain. One man near Plankinton threshed 4,400 bushels of barley from an eighty-acre field last week. J. A. Moon, living south of here, has a field of wheat that shocked fifty-four shocks of twelve largest sized harvester bundles each, to the acre. J. R. Mabbot, east of town, has a seventy-acre field of wheat that made 3,150 twelve bundle shocks. In very many cases harvesters were abandoned for headers, as the grain was too heavy to bind. Most of the grain in this section was saved—very little of it being lodged.. This is very fortunate, too, as many fields of oats stood from four to five and a half feet in height. Plankinton people propose to celebrate the grand harvest by having a grain palace to be opened from September 29 to October 3d inclusive.

Corn is growing finely, and almost every farmer in Aurora county has had roasting ears out of his own corn-field. The Alliance supply house here ran short of twine several days since. The cause, as given by Manager Locke, is that where from one pound to one and a half pounds has been sufficient to bind wheat heretofore, it takes two to three and a half pounds this year. One farmer, living north of Plankinton, used 225 pounds of twine to bind 100 acres of wheat.

Dick McAndu, an Aurora county farmer, filled two header boxes in cutting eighty rods on his barley field. He took this to a machine, threshing in a neighboring field, and threshed forty-seven bushels of barley from the two boxes.

Mr. Snow, of Palatine township, from two and a half acres threshed 100 bushels of wheat. Here is 40 bushels to the acre and can be supported by affidavits. A man who would kick at this kind of farming would turn up his nose at a gold mine.

B. V. & J. L. Cook, of Palatine township, threshed from 16 acres, 675 bushels of wheat, machine measure, which will grade No. 1 northern. This is an average of 43 bushels to the acre.

Brule County, South Dakota.

Brule County is situated on the eastern side of the Missouri river, Chamberlain being the county seat and the gateway to the Sioux Reservation.

The soil of Brule county is a rich, black, sandy loam, from one to three feet deep, with a clay subsoil; it is easily worked, very productive, and one of the best of soils for the retention of moisture.

The products grown here are all that are grown in the eastern and middle states. They ordinarily yield well, and in numerous cases extra large crops are raised. The fact is apparent here as elsewhere that good farming pays best.

There are several creeks and lakes in different parts of the county, affording excellent stock water in their localities. Where wells are dug, water is usually found at from 10 to 60 feet, and is of good quality.

The climate is mild and pleasant, and the winters are not so severe and hard to bear as in some localities where the atmosphere is more moist and where the mercury does not reach so low a point.

The Chicago, Milwaukee & St. Paul Railway crosses the state from east to west, giving railway connections with the eastern markets.

The county has a population of about 8,000, composed almost entirely of people from the eastern states. They are an active and energetic class of people and are fast making Brule one of the first counties in the state.

Brule is one of the "banner counties" of the state as regards her schools. All through the county one passes neat school buildings, nicely painted and kept in good repair.

In the towns of Chamberlain, Pukwana and Kimball there are graded schools, with an efficient corps of teachers.

There are in the county at the present time several different church organizations, including Baptist, Methodist, Congregationalist, Presbyterian, Lutheran and Catholic. Most of the denominations have churches in Chamberlain and Kimball, with pastors located there. There are also different organizations throughout the county that hold their services in some of the numerous school houses, supplied with a pastor from the neighboring towns.

Brule county has soil that will raise crops of all descriptions in abundance. This season the wheat crop will average about 20 bushels per acre, throughout the county.

Corn has never been better than at the present time, yielding about 60 bushels per acre. Oats, barley, rye and other grains have grown luxuriantly; their yield is large and quality good. In vegetables we can show as good quality and as large variety as any county in South Dakota.

All kinds of stock do well. Horses, cattle and sheep thrive and fatten on the native grasses, and annually thousands of tons of hay go to waste. At any time during the winter when the ground is free from snow, stock will keep in good condition without feeding hay or grain. Large numbers of hogs are raised and marketed from this county, and such a thing as disease is almost unknown among live stock of all kinds. The soil and climate of the county are such as to adapt it to farming and stock raising. The price of land at this time is very low, and in many cases this year's crop has yielded a return to the producer that would pay for the land it was grown upon three or four times over. To all parties desiring to invest or secure homes, we would say see Brule county before you locate, and you will be convinced that there is no place in the northwest where your money will bring you surer returns, or where you can secure a good home on as favorable terms.

NEWSPAPER ITEMS.

Chamberlain Democrat: A. B. Ayres, of Lyman, in the ceded Sioux lands, this year has raised ten acres of broom corn. Many of the stalks are over eleven feet in height. Mr. Ayres has raised broom corn for thirty years, and previous to coming here had a broom factory in Kansas. He declares that the broom corn raised by him this year is the best that he has ever seen. About the 15th of September, when the corn is dry, he will engage a place here and manufacture brooms.

John Wilkes, of Plummer township, was in the city the end of the week. He informed us that he has 40 acres of millet which he estimates will yield fully 4 tons to the acre. Mr. Wilkes has great faith in the sheep industry, and two years ago purchased 170 sheep. The increase the first year was 145. This year's increase is 200. Since the first purchase, he has bought 171—118 recently and the remaining 53 last year. He has sold about 65, leaving a total of over 600. From wool, sheep and lambs sold he has realized the snug sum of $670.

SIOUX RESERVATION.

The Great Sioux Reservation is in the corn belt of South Dakota, and was opened for settlement in the year 1890.

There are 3,000,000 acres of choice and fertile lands open to settlement, much of which has running water and timber upon it. Any citizen who has never used his homestead right can secure 160 acres of this choice land by paying the filing fee of $14.00 and residing upon the land for fourteen months, at which time, should the settler choose to do so, he can make final proof by paying the government price—$1.25 per acre—or he can reside upon the land for seven years without making proof, and thereby avoid paying taxes—as land, the title of which is still in the United States, is not taxable.

The county of Lyman, just west of Chamberlain, has a population of about 150 people. This county has about sixty miles fronting on the Missouri River and passing through the southern part of it is the White River, with several small creeks running into each of the above rivers. The above mentioned county contains about twenty-four civil townships. The county of Presho, adjoining Lyman on the west, contains about the same area and the same number of inhabitants. The county of Pratt, being still west of Presho county, has quite a number of settlers located within its boundaries. The placid waters of White River and Medicine Creek flow through the southern and central parts of these counties. Homesteads can still be secured in these counties with running water and timber on them, good hay land, and the soil is very fertile, being a dark, rich, sandy loam with a clay subsoil.

Still west of the above come Jackson and Nowlin counties, each having quite a number of settlers located within their limits and both have the White and Bad Rivers with their tributaries running through them. Good water can be secured on the table or prairie lands, in either of the above counties, by digging wells ranging in depth from ten to sixty feet. All the settlers who located in time to plant crops in the spring of 1891 have been favored with fine returns; wheat, although sown in small tracts, yielded this season (1891) from 16 to 24 bushels per acre, oats from 30 to 60, sod corn from 15 to 35 bushels per acre, and vegetables equally well.

CHAMBERLAIN is the gateway to the Sioux Reservation.

Bon Homme County, South Dakota.

Benj. Bussey lives one mile from Tyndall in Bon Homme county. Mr. B. opened the farm thirteen years ago when he did not have a dollar in cash to his name—only a good team, a few tools, a pair of willing hands and a contented and cheerful spirit. Now he owns 400 acres of land clear of all encumbrances, 105 head of cattle, 275 hogs, 17 horses, excellent buildings and a two-inch artesian well which furnishes plenty of good water for the house and barns, and light power for grinding, churning, etc. He has 31 varieties of fruit—12 being of apples which he planted in 1879. His success with small fruits has been abundant. Last Wednesday he hauled 80 bushels of apples to the market at Tyndall, for which he received one dollar per bushel, and still has 300 bushels at home which he will dispose of as occasion permits at good advantage. Another thing: Mr. Bussey now cuts all his fuel from a 10 acre grove which he set out and cultivated with his own hands.

This is only one among a hundred similar cases which could be mentioned for Bon Homme county.

Charles Mix County, South Dakota.

NEWSPAPER ITEMS.

Castalia Record: Henry Emery brought in two samples of alfalfa raised on his Snake Creek farm. The older specimen was two feet and a half high and was cut in the early part of June. The other was the second growth on the same field and was equally as high as the first crop. Mr. Emery thinks he will yet have another crop, making the third harvest from the same field in one season. It yields about five tons to the acre at each cutting. A farmer with whom we were conversing recently regarding crops, made the assertion that the cash realized on a field of wheat this year would more than pay for the land the grain grew on. It is a fact that a few farms in this county can be bought for less money than this year's crop will be worth, but it is also true that such will not be the case in a short time from now. Eastern farmers will never find a better time than the present to invest in Charles Mix county land. We have a stalk of corn on exhibition at this office that measures eleven feet and two inches high. It has two long ears at a height of two feet and a half from the ground. Louis Garrl, who brought it in, says he has seven acres like it. It was raised on the river bottom, southwest.

Edgerton News: Don't seem reasonable, does it? It is a fact, nevertheless, that farms can be bought in this vicinity for $1,000 to $1,200, the crops from which will sell for $1,200 to $1,600. These farms will raise just as big crops next year as they have this year. Why not? There has been enough wheat threshed in Charles Mix county so that we can place the average yield pretty accurately. It will be twenty-five bushels per acre the county over.

Bloomington Courier: There is hardly a farmer in Charles Mix county who could not start a bank this fall, and a good many of them are going to buy a lot of shares in the banks which are being incorporated. Still we have room for more farmers to make just the same kind of a start.

W. H. Ellis of Castalia, Charles Mix county, has a faith in South Dakota and Charles Mix county born of experience with other portions of the world and of practical knowledge. He has made a close calculation of the yield of agricultural products in Charles Mix county this year and the figures are these:

There were 24,000 acres sown to wheat in Charles Mix County this year. The yield will be an average of twenty-five bushels to the acre or 600,000 bushels.

There are 40,000 acres of corn to yield forty bushels to the acre or 1,600,000. There are 4,000 acres of flax which will yield 15 bushels per acre, or 60,000 bushels.

There are 5,000 head of cattle and 9,000 hogs to be marketed.

Wheat will sell at 90 cents per bushel, corn at 25 cents per bushel, flax $1.00 per bushel, cattle will be worth an average of $25.00 per head and hogs $8.00 each. The value of the crop at these figures will be $1,147,000.

This is an average of $225 for each one of the 5,000 people in Charles Mix, or 1,000 for each of the 1,000 voters in that county. It will cost $6,000 to get this crop to market. It will be marketed at Kimball or Armour.

J. C. McLain has 542 bushels of wheat, 210 of oats, 65 of rye, 71 of barley, and 28 acres of the best corn he ever produced, as the result of his summer's work with one very light team. And not a dollar's expense except for twine and threshing bill.

Davison County, South Dakota.

NEWSPAPER ITEMS.

Mail: It took one-half day to thresh the wheat from 20 acres on Jake Johnson's farm, three miles northwest of Mt. Vernon. It yielded 37½ bushels to the acre. Ransom Malde, three miles east of Mt. Vernon, rejoices because his 50 acres of wheat poured out 33½ bushels to the acre. John E. Good, of Badger township, thinks he can go the heavy yielder one better. He measured off two acres of ground and threshed the wheat on it. The result was 72 bushels by exact weight. He has 69 acres left, better than the sample. He says he gets more by this one wheat crop than all the land and buildings thereon are worth. He has a big corn crop out of reach of the frost.

Letcher Blade: Hardman and Mildenberger threshed 9 acres of oats Tuesday afternoon for Henry Hopkins, which yielded 618 bushels, machine measure, a little over 68 bushels per acre. They threshed 30 acres of wheat for A. H. Locke, of Blendon, which gave 25 bushels per acre, and another small field of 2 acres which yielded 32 bushels per acre. Mr. Wallace, of Perry, 1,100 bushels of wheat from 40 acres and 420 bushels from 14 acres.

George Watson, of Prosper, returned from Sioux City where he turned off $700 worth of choice cattle at good prices.

W. C. Russ calculates that he could fill twenty cars with the product of his farm this season, including wheat, oats, squashes, pumpkins, hay, etc.

John Wilkinson brings in some fine samples of corn from his farm near Emsley. The ears measured 13 inches in length and 8 inches in circumference. He has 30 acres which he says will yield 70 bushels per acre.

C. W. Kellie, of Mt. Vernon, writes that oats are going from 50 to 100 bushels per acre, barley from 25 to 60, and other grains in proportion. He says there will be 300,000 bushels marketed at that place this season.

A bunch of wheat is on exhibition in this office from the farm of F. B. Angell, southeast of town, that is an eye-opener. The heads are fully 6 inches long and filled with plump grains to the very tip. Mr. Angell figures on 30 bushels to the acre, but his neighbors put it as high as 36.

John Schmidt, of Beulah Township, threshed 1,062 bushels of oats from 28 acres, and 500 of wheat from 19 acres, with 30 acres more to thresh. He sold 500 bushels of wheat Saturday at 74 cents, and 500 bushels of oats at 20 cents.

Levi Brown, of Rome, threshed 20 acres of oats which went 70 bushels, machine measure, and 83 bushels by weight. His wheat went 15 bushels and his corn promises 60 to 75. Mrs. David Cole got 378 bushels of wheat off 15 acres, and John Vogu's wheat went 24 bushels.

Mark Scott, from Sault Ste. Marie, an old friend of landlord Simpson, of the south side, has removed to this city to make it his home. Mr. Scott has a fine farm just over the line in Hanson county, which has been rented for several years and on which he has not had anything like a failure. He has devoted the past year to traveling over the Northwest, through Montana, Idaho, Washington and Oregon, and is perfectly satisfied to locate in South Dakota.

F. B. Angell, of Prosper, who is one of the most systematic and successful of Davison county farmers, has brought in a sample of apples raised on his place that compare very favorably with those shipped in from Iowa and Missouri, and demonstrate beyond a doubt that this can be made a fruit raising country. One of the apples measures 11¼ inches in circumference and the other 10¾, there being six trees of this variety, fairly loaded down. Mr. Angell has besides this variety 100 trees of other kinds, all well laden with fruit.

J. W. Ottman was in from Rome Saturday. He says B. S. Barnard had 70 acres of wheat that went 27 bushels, while his oats turned out 45 bushels. One of the most remarkable growths of the year is that of a rose bush in the yard of Mr. Mutzger, of Ethan, which, by actual measurement, has grown 11 feet.

Douglas County, South Dakota.
NEWSPAPER ITEMS.

Armour Tribune: A short ride northeast of Armour shows as good crops as are found in any part of the county. E. E. Sisson has a model farm throughout. Nice residence, barn, pastures and a field that gave forth a bountiful yield. And, too, one would think that Hawley Bros. farmed most of Douglas county, should you attempt to drive around their extensive farm. Then Carl Shroeder has a fine place, with his large, white farm house surrounded by a beautiful grove. Carl expects to sell this year over $4,000 worth of farm products from his 300 acres of land. One does not realize how Douglas county has improved until a drive through the county opens the eyes to that fact. John M. Hammond had a mammoth turnip on exhibition at his store August 1. The turnip weighed 4¾ pounds and measured 24½ inches in circumference.

Armour Tribune: We cannot get through shouting for Douglas county crops. Chas. P. Smith has an eight acre field that yielded him 318 bushels of wheat.

Hanson County, South Dakota.
NEWSPAPER ITEMS.

W. F. Loomer rented his farm in Edgerton two years ago and last year he received $200 clear, which was about 13 per cent. on $2,000, the price of his farm. This year he says his half of the crop will net him over $1,000.

C. L. Holbrook, who reported 26½ acres of wheat as yielding 41 bushels per acre, has finished 100 acres yielding 3,700 bushels.

Alexandria Journal: Thousands of tons of excellent hay will go to waste in this county because of big crop. A few hay presses could be made to pay if the proper parties took hold of the matter.

M. Johnston's wheat went over 25 bushels to the acre; he will have 1,000 bushels when it is all threshed. Mr. Johnston put the wheat in himself, and this is pretty good for a man 70 years old.

C. L. Holbrook had close to 100 acres of wheat which yielded 3,700 bushels. 27 acres, nearly, gave an average of 40½ bushels to the acre, machine measure. So far this is the banner yield of the county.

Slade Bros. threshed 100 acres of wheat, average 30 bushels to the acre. They have a good many acres left that will go at least 30 bushels to the acre, as it is much better than what was threshed. Their barley went 63 bushels to the acre.

J. P. Nissen's barley went 82 bushels to the acre.

G. D. Peck's wheat threshed out 34 bushels to the acre.

Henry Jensen got 40 bushels of wheat per acre from 11 acres.

Frank Morse threshed 20 acres of wheat which went 38 bushels to the acre.

R. Houge had a stack of grain in which there were only four loads; when threshed it yielded 100 bushels.

Fred Brande is in good shape. About 50 acres of wheat yielded 1,246 bushels, 25 to the acre; 13½ acres of oats, 670 bushels, 50 to the acre; 10 acres of barley, 300 bushels, 30 to the acre; 20 acres of rye, 445 bushels, 22 to the acre.

Erick Thompson measured off 3½ acres of wheat land and had the wheat on it threshed. It yielded 130 bushels, an average of 39 bushels to the acre. This was his best looking wheat. The rest will not go over 30 bushels to the acre.

Robert Gingles threshed 25 acres of wheat that went 39 bushels to the acre.

Tom Smith, of Springlake township, threshed 60 acres of wheat getting 29¼ bushels to the acre. The wheat was sold bringing him in clean cash $1,285.

Hutchinson County, South Dakota.
NEWSPAPER ITEMS.

Charles Holten threshed over 1,100 bushels of barley off 20 acres, an average of nearly 57 bushels to the acre. The first threshing of wheat in this township yielded 36 bushels to the acre. Asa Brink, of Milltown, marketed over $400 worth of hogs here Thursday last. Jacob Rapp run out one field of oats which averaged 88 bushels to the acre. F. B. Gage brought in a bunch of barley, the heads of which are all five inches long, not including the beards. Representative Kline also comes to the front with a good crop. He could not cut his grain last week by taking a full swath. The binder was turning all the time on the machine, but it could not make the bundles as fast as they rolled up. Frederick Heintz, a farmer living south of town, off 10 acres got 360 bushels of wheat, machine measure.

Parkston Advance: Jacob Rapp threshed 1,490 bushels of oats from 52 acres, being 67 bushels to the acre. The sacks which held two bushels only held three half bushel measures at the machine, so it is safe to say he got 80 to 90 bushels to the acre.

Advance: John Fish threshed his wheat and averaged about 20 bushels to the acre. Mr. Isaac Stainbrook brought in a fine sample of flint corn. The ears averaged a foot in length. A lady brought Grimm & Co. a load of cabbages last week which averaged 13½ pounds each. The vegetable is still growing, and the krout supply can surely not be short this year.

The following items taken from The Advance will prove very distinctly that Hutchinson county falls in line with the other counties surrounding it in producing the largest fruit and crop yield of any section or state of the Union:

Harvey Hipple mowed 10 acres of millet the other day which will yield about 25 tons of choice hay.

Bares & Faust threshed 230 bushels of wheat in one hour for John Cremer.

Charlie Kreier, living on the Osborn farm, threshed 1,007 bushels of wheat and 400 bushels of oats.

Floy B. Gage got 490 bushels of barley from 20 acres of land. His oats averaged about 50 bushels to the acre. Russel Gage got 55 bushels to the acre.

Rev. C. B. Clarke returned from Salem where he conducted services yesterday. He counted 1,300 stacks of grain between the towns of Spencer and Salem, which are ten miles apart.

Charles J. Ohlson, of Union township, had 64 acres of wheat that turned out 2,050 bushels, an average of nearly 40 bushels per acre.

Geo. Schilling brought in a fine sample of corn of flint variety which is very fine indeed, the ears being 15 inches in length.

W. C. Nye reports having threshed a field of wheat that yielded 40 bushels per acre. The more threshing that is being done the higher the average yield for the county goes. From reports received up to date the average yield in the county is above 25 bushels.

Ebenezer Johnson, of Jackson, threshed out 121 bushels of oats from 1½ acres. He says had the oats not fallen down so they could not be reached by the binder, he would have had 100 bushels on an acre. As it is, his 15 acres will yield him 1,000 bushels or more.

Mrs. H. E. Hipple, living about two miles southeast of town, has gathered her apple crop, and says from 6 trees she will get about 10 bushels of fine apples. It is the first year they have had any as their trees are young, but this speaks for itself that fruit can be raised in abundance in this country.

Mrs. J. H. Reynolds brings in some fine apples which were raised on her farm near the Hanson county line. She has a number of trees, all of which are loaded with fruit, and some of the limbs were broken off by the weight of the apples.

Jerauld County, South Dakota.

Jerauld county, along the line of the Firesteel Valley, has perhaps some of the most remarkable yields of any in the state, only a few of which can be given here:

Frank Brown, who lives west of Wessington Springs, threshed two fields of wheat that yielded 33 bushels and 38 bushels respectively.

C. L. Holbrook, of Wessington Springs, threshed 27 acres that averaged 41½ bushels per acre and 35 acres that yielded 34¼ bushels per acre, machine measure, the former weighing out 45 bushels at the elevator.

W. S. Arnold, on the farm of D. A. Scott, near Wessington Springs, threshed out 139 acres that averaged 33⅓ bushels per acre.

Senator Smith, of Wessington Springs, has 27 acres that he is confident will weigh out when threshed 50 bushels per acre, a little of it threshed measured out 49 bushels.

J. A. Holcomb, Wessington Springs, S. D., threshed out 3,000 bush. from 100 acres.

Chas. Walters, living 12 miles west of Woonsocket, in Viola township, will have 4,000 bushels of No. 1 hard, this season; 70 acres of what he has threshed yielded a trifle over 40 bushels per acre.

Many farmers who offered their farms a year ago for a nominal sum **have raised wheat enough alone this year to buy two or three more farms just like them.**

Alpena Journal, Aug. 21: Dell Leighton sowed on Chas. Haskin's farm, south of town, twelve acres of wheat, and the same was threshed last Saturday and marketed the same day, the gross weight being 24,735 pounds or 412½ bushels, being over 34 bushels per acre.

Lake County, South Dakota.
NEWSPAPER ITEMS.

Madison Sentinel: A. E. Hill, half acre—19 bushels and a peck of wheat tested 60 pounds strong.

W. A. Porteus, near Ramona—125 acres yielded 3,250 bushels of wheat—26 bushels even to the acre.

Ferguson Bros., of Wayne township, 200 acres of wheat threshed out 5,300 bushels.

Joseph Hiller, of Concord township, has threshed out 12 acres of wheat on measured ground, that weighed out 40 bushels to the acre.

Adolph Schmidt, Farmington township, had 31 acres of wheat that threshed out 940 bushels.

H. G. Mueller, Farmington, 20 acres of flax yielded 300 bushels.

W. A. Porteus, living north of this city, has threshed out a portion of his wheat crop—125 acres—from which he secured 3,250 bushels, or 26 bushels to the acre, and the farms of his neighbors will yield fully as well. Miles McLeod has threshed 100 acres of wheat on his farm in the western portion of the county, from which he measures up 2,300 bushels. He has 150 acres of fine flax and 50 acres of oats that will shell out 60 bushels to the acre. These are but a few samples of what the Lake county harvest will average. The grain, too, is of a very fine quality; the berry is large and plump.

The Syd Dakota Ekko tells of a man named Anderson, who lives near Madison, and is the owner of a 600-acre farm. He recently threshed 26,000 bushels of wheat, an average of 43⅓ bushels per acre, with a weight of 61 pounds to the bushel. Can any other state beat it?

McCook County, South Dakota.
NEWSPAPER ITEMS.

Pioneer Register: The Register editor accompanied J. C. Headlee on a drive through the country Tuesday of this week. We put in a whole day, going first northwest through Pearle township and came back south of Spencer. It is a time of year when farmers are very busy, but one can discern that they work with a greater vim than usual, and it is well they might, for they have one of the finest harvests that ever blessed the tiller of the soil, and consequently are encouraged in exerting their physical as well as mental abilities. Everything seemed to be humming; some were still running their binders, tying up the golden sheafs of their late grain, while others were stacking, plowing or making hay.

The thickness of the shocks show a heavy growth of straw, and all one has to do is to lift up a bundle to be convinced that it was necessary for a rank growth to bear up the well filled heads of plump wheat and oats. The recent rains have filled up all the low places and lake beds, and put the ground in good condition for fall plowing. With the ground well soaked, as it is now, and the numerous bodies of water, which will tend to draw moisture, it seems that the rain fall and proper moisture would surely be settled for next year.

Here's a straight tip to some of the eastern farmers. L. Johnson, who lives just north of this place, commenced work on his farm the 10th day of April last. He did not have a furrow turned, but commenced his fall plowing. He planted his own crop and did all the work of his farm, besides exchanging work with his neighbors to secure all his help during threshing time. As a result of his labors, on September 2, less than a period of five months, he had housed safely in his granaries on his farm the following cereals: Wheat, 1,300 bushels; oats, 1,500 bushels; barley, 300 bushels, and flax, 175 bushels; making a grand total of 3,275 bushels. In addition to this he has 40 acres of late corn and a field of late flax and millet yet to hear from. We have no doubt that there are farmers in this county who have far excelled Mr. Johnson, but this is given as a sample of what can be accomplished by intelligent and industrious work by farmers in South Dakota. He has good farm machinery and did all the work in the planting and growing of the above crop with the aid of only one team of horses in the time intervening between April 10 and September 2. With the present good prices for grain this is a good summer's work. A farmer is truly a king in South Dakota. The men who are renting farms in the east can come out here and buy a farm and in a couple of years pay for all of it and own it, if they were to hustle like Mr. Johnson.

Miner County, South Dakota.
NEWSPAPER ITEMS.

Fall plowing has commenced and the ground is in excellent condition. Hundreds of acres which have not been cultivated since the drought of 1889 will be plowed and put in condition for a crop next year, and no land will remain uncultivated here in 1892. During the past three years it has been difficult to obtain renters for land, but this bountiful harvest is bringing quite a large number of people looking for lands to rent. Our numerous artesian wells are quite an inducement to renters who have farmed in localities where water had to be hauled for all purposes. Nearly every quarter section in the southwest portion of the county has a flowing well on it and others are being bored, so we shall soon have the best watered county in the state.

Following is a list of a few farmers who have threshed their 1891 crops:

Charles Larson, 496 bushels of wheat from 16 acres.

Herman Hanneman, 1,400 bushels of wheat from 50 acres.

John Streigel, 668 bushels of wheat from 30 acres, 500 bushels wheat from 16 acres.

John J. Langland, 1,114 bushels of wheat from 44 acres, 680 bushels of oats from 16 acres.

Chas. Gehring, 940 bushels of wheat from 35 acres.

F. C. Wescott, 976 bushels of wheat from 33 acres.

S. S. Russell, 1,180 bushels of wheat from 62 acres, 558 bushels of barley from 22 acres.

V. D. Smith, 493 bushels of wheat from 23 acres.

John Mahony, 198 bushels of barley from 5 acres.

Boyd McVety, 700 bushels of wheat from 25 acres.

Anton Kuhle, 895 bushels of wheat from 30 acres.

Sam Suffron, 864 bushels of oats from 12 acres, 248 bushels of barley from 4 acres, 1,050 bushels of wheat from 50 acres.

C. A. Crissey, 1,420 bushels of wheat from 90 acres, 237 bushels of rye from 15 acres, 500 bushels of oats from 20 acres.

Dan Mahony, 1,450 bushels of wheat from 80 acres, 300 bushels of flax from 30 acres, 404 bushels of oats from 10 acres.

J. J. Cox, 1,200 bushels of wheat from 65 acres, 140 bushels of flax from 12 acres, 450 bushels of barley from 14 acres.

G. M. Farley, 950 bushels of wheat from 40 acres.

C. J. Henderson, 845 bushels of wheat from 40 acres.

Sanborn County, South Dakota.
NEWSPAPER ITEMS.

Woonsocket Special: This portion of South Dakota is in the midst of the most abundant harvest known in years, if, indeed, ever equalled. It is now believed by the best and most conservative judges that the average of the entire county will not be less than 20 bushels per acre. There are many fields that will reach 30 and even 35 bushels per acre. Oats are beyond question unprecedented. The yield will average about 50 bushels to the acre. Where it took from a pound to a pound and a half of twine per acre in former years, farmers are this year using from two and a half to three pounds per acre on an average, while four pounds are used by many and five pounds for oats. A sample of oats measuring over five feet and having heads a foot long is on exhibition here. It is only an average of a large field which is estimated to yield 70 to 100 bushels per acre. This is an exception, of course, but the writer has seen many fields that will yield 60 to 65 bushels per acre, not in small areas, but in fields of from 20 to 80 acres.

Artesian Advocate: A. F. Kelly has threshed, and finds that from 105 acres he raised 2,783 bushels of wheat, an average of 26½ bushels per acre. His oats 55 bushels. On a piece that yielded 29 bushels of wheat per acre he says he sowed hardly a bushel to the acre. On an average he sowed about 1½ bushels to the acre. W. S. Hibbard raised 692 bushels of wheat from 32 acres, which is a yield of nearly 22 bushels per acre. Hans Williamson raised 17 acres of wheat. The yield per acre ranged from 23 to 28 bushels. Geo. G. Watkins threshed from one acre 36 bushels of wheat.

Letcher Blade: We want to give the record of a man who lives five miles east of this place. His name is Alphonso Van Overschelde and his address is Letcher.
Four years ago he worked as a farm hand for Chas. Blanchard, for $18 a month.
Three years ago he bought 160 acres of land for $850, mortgaged for $500.
Two years ago he bought another farm of 160 acres for $1,000, mortgaged for $500.
One year ago he bought still another for $950, mortgaged for $500.
This year he put down an artesian well on one of these places at a cost of about $500.
He raised on this land this year: 190 acres wheat, 3,000 bushels; 100 acres corn, 2,500 bushels; 50 acres flax, 500 bushels; 40 acres oats, 2,400 bushels.
Calling the wheat worth 85 cents, the corn 25, the flax 85 and the oats 20, his crop this year will yield $4,000. That is, the crop of one season pays the entire cost of the farms on which it was raised and leaves $1,200 in the treasury.

A. F. Kelley, Woonsocket, S. D., 100 acres of hard wheat averaged 27½ bushels.

Charles Olson, P. O. Forrestburg, threshed 55 acres that yielded 36 2-5 bushels per acre.

Jas. Harris, Forrestburg, raised 32 bushels of wheat per acre.

Geo. Simms, P. O. Woonsocket, S. D., raised 47½ acres of wheat that averaged 27 bushels per acre.

W. G. Santee, Forrestburg P. O., S. D., had 17 acres of hard wheat that threshed 611 bushels, or about 36 bushels per acre.

Hiram Rhodee, of Forrestburg, S. D., had 8 acres of wheat that threshed 40 bushels per acre; his average on 60 acres was 26 bushels.

Andrew C. Scott, of Artesian, threshed out 30 acres of wheat that went 29 bushels per acre.

Chas. Bechtold, P. O. Woonsocket, threshed out 33 acres that averaged 28 bushels per acre.

Chas. Grissell, of Woonsocket, put in 25 acres of stubble on the farm of Judge Reed, three miles south of town, this year, by simply pulverizing it once over, putting the 25 acres in one day; he threshed 625 bushels from this field, an average of 25 bush. per acre.

Turner County, South Dakota.
NEWSPAPER ITEMS.

Turner County Herald: T. R. Negus reports threshing 38 acres of wheat which went 25 bushels to the acre.

Ed. Basye threshed last week and the yields were: Oats, 60 bushels per acre; wheat, 25 bushels; flax, 14 bushels.

Jos. Andrews reports from Spring Valley that what wheat he has threshed on his farm goes 27 bushels to the acre.

Mr. A. Schnose, four miles east of town, threshed 570 bushels of wheat from 19 acres, and 810 bushels of oats from 13 acres.

Wm. Johnkes, living on J. T. Hogan's farm in Spring Valley, threshed this week, the yield being: Wheat, 28 bushels; oats, 75; flax, 11½.

John Lease, who purchased the Wormwood farm, two miles northwest of Hurley, last year, says that his rent for the same (one-third of the crop) will amount to one-half of the purchase price of the farm.

Hans Sorensen, in section 20, twp. 97, range 54—Swan Lake—threshed this week and received 120 bushels of wheat from 3 acres of ground. His oats, 6¼ acres, yielded 518 bushels, nearly 82¾ bushels to the acre.

Yankton County, South Dakota.

Capitalists, manufacturers and farmers will find no better location to engage in business for profit than in Yankton county. To the residents of the eastern states who are looking westward, a special invitation is extended. We have many advantages to offer. To the manufacturer we offer cheap power; and we have raw materials for many kinds of manufacturing. To the capitalist there is unlimited field for investment, and to the farmer we offer superior advantages. Here his products are two-fold greater, the price as good, and the profits double those of eastern farms. Land here can be bought for $10 to $15 an acre. This is an old but not thickly settled county, and the social, religious and educational advantages are far in advance of most western communities. District schools are held in neat school houses on an average of nine months in the year in the country, while Yankton city schools enjoys an unsurpassed graded school system, employing twenty teachers and occupying three fine brick school buildings. Higher education is afforded by Yankton College, where a regular college course is taught.

Yankton county is in the extreme southern part of South Dakota, and in substantially the same latitude as Buffalo, New York. It lies in the valley of the Missouri and also in that of the Dakota or James river, which unites with the Missouri river about ten miles east of the city of Yankton. Although the county lies thus in two great valleys, but very little of it consists of what is generally known as "waste-land." It is most beautiful rolling prairie, with now and then a stream of water or a little lake, and is remarkably free from waste land, whether of swamps, slough or bluffs. The soil is deep loam, strong, warm and quick, dries quickly on the surface, but holds moisture below, and being underlaid by a clay subsoil, is capable of withstanding droughts, which in other countries would render a crop impossible. All kinds of vegetables, wheat, oats, flax, clover and tame grasses are cultivated with great success, while corn is a sure crop. Corn is rapidly becoming the principal crop in this region. During the last five seasons the yield has been large, the quality excellent, and thousands of bushels of it have been sold in Illinois and Iowa for planting. With corn and hay in abundance, the raising of cattle and hogs has become a safe and profitable branch of farming. Sheep are also raised with profit, the wool finding a home market at the Woolen Mill in Yankton. Good water is abundant and can be obtained in wells of moderate depth. Nowhere in the west can there be found more desirable lands than the 350,000 acres within the limits of Yankton county. In this county the lands are cheaper than in many others, notwithstanding the fact that the price of real estate has nearly doubled during the last two years. The eminent success gained by many farmers in Yankton county is abundant evidence of what can be done. It is cheaper to buy a farm in Yankton county than to take up Government land.

YANKTON, August 22, 1891.

I came to Yankton in 1874 and have lived here ever since. I have controlled and had cultivated and farmed a good many acres of land. I have represented 500 to 1500 acres per year, and I find that when proper care is taken to till the soil, that a crop is certain. I have also discovered that there is but one month in the year to break new lands and that is June. Breaking in any other month does not rot, hence in dry seasons you cannot look for good crops. Good many have raised flax on breaking, but it is best not to do so, better let the breaking rest and rot; sub-soil in the fall, sow to wheat or oats in the following spring, and after that with deep plowing, and in dry seasons put your grain in with drill, and you will be satisfied with your crops, as the sun cannot dry the roots, and the good dews we have in Dakota will certainly produce good results. In almost all new countries, breaking is done in all seasons of the year, it does not rot and is always raw and grassy, and does not produce anything in a dry season, while in a wet season a fair crop is raised, but never half as good as crops on breaking done in June. This is the reason largely that Yankton county has never had a crop failure, as she is an old county and the ground is in good shape to retain moisture, hence we never have any trouble with crops. My farms have all been worked by tenants, and they average usually as follows: Wheat, 15 to 25; oats, 35 to 60; and all other crops in proportion. I have traveled and lived in most of the states of the Union, and prefer South Dakota, taking everything into consideration. Shall be pleased to answer any information.

P. O. Box 606.   G. W. ROBERTS.

Yankton Press: Steven Cummins, just east of Gayville, 40 acres of oats yielded 2,600 bushels machine measure; over 3,000 bushels by weight.

Charles Chippery, 4 acres of barley, threshed 228 bushels, 57 bushels to the acre.

J. H. Mileage, on the Gayville road, 100 acres of oats, 7,500 bushels, machine measure; weighed over 7,000 bushels.

C. Volin, 15 acres of wheat, 37 bushels to the acre; 22 acres o oats, 70 bushels to the acre, machine measure.

The Jim Robb farm run by Smith: 125 acres of wheat, 30 bushels to the acre, 75 acres of oats, 65 bushels to the acre, machine measure.

A. Berkley, 12 acres of wheat, 450 bushels, about 37½ bushels to the acre.

Wm. F. Lawrence, 65 acres of oats, 5,000 bushels, or 76 bushels to the acre. This must be among the best in the county for a large acreage.

Will Temple's barley threshed out 45 bushels to the acre.

The Johnson boys near H. H. Smith's farm realized 50 bushels of barley to the acre.

D. O. Lawrence, 4 acres of wheat yielded 200 bushels, or 50 bushels to the acre, and 30 acres of wheat yielded 1,110 bushels, about 37 bushels to the acre.

John Calmer's oats yielded from 75 to 80 bushels to the acre.

The Great Northwest.
Figures that show its Truly Wonderful Growth.

The Harvest Festival in Minneapolis was made the occasion, by The Tribune of that city, of presenting some facts and figures about the great Northwest that are of interest: In 1850 there were in the territory of Minnesota—now the hard wheat belt, including the states of Minnesota, North and South Dakota, and parts of Wyoming and Montana, 6,077 souls.

The total agricultural operations of this vast section—over three times the size of England—were conducted on 157 farms, with $15,000 worth of farm machinery, 430 span of horses, 325 yokes of oxen and 14 mules.

The total agricultural productions of the hard wheat belt in 1850 were as follows: 1,401 bushels of wheat, 125 bushels of rye, 16,725 bushels of corn, 30,582 bushels of oats, 1,216 bushels of barley, 515 bushels of buckwheat, 10,002 bushels of beans, 21,145 bushels of potatoes, 2,019 tons of hay, 1,100 pounds of butter, 2,950 pounds of maple sugar, 85 pounds of wool and 80 pounds of honey.

In 1850 the wheat product of the Northwest hard wheat belt was 1,401 bushels, in 1891, 150,000,000 bushels.

In 1860 the Dakotas produced 900 bushels of wheat; in 1891, 90,000,000 bushels. There were under cultivation in the three hard wheat states in 1850, 5,000 acres all told. In 1891 there were 15,000,000 acres planted to wheat, corn and oats alone.

The farms which were valued at $161,000 in 1850 are valued to-day at over $500,000,000. As late as 1870 the farms of diminutive Rhode Island were worth ten times the farms of the two Dakotas, while the farms of Ohio were worth ten times the farms of Minnesota and the Dakotas combined. Even in 1880 the Dakotas possessed only a little more than one-half as many farms as Connecticut, and produced only one-third as much wheat as the little Southern state of Maryland. But in 1891, North Dakota, single-handed, not only tills more soil than Maryland, but produces more wheat than the entire "solid South."

In 1860 Minnesota had under cultivation less acres than Delaware; in 1891, nearly as many acres as all New England. The farms of Minnesota in 1860 were worth only one-third the farms of Connecticut; but the Minnesota crop of 1891 will buy every farm, farm building and implement in the Nutmeg state. In 1860 Minnesota raised less corn than Delaware, less wheat than Georgia and one-half as much oats as New Jersey. In 1891 Minnesota harvested five times as many acres of wheat alone as the six states of New England planted in wheat, corn and oats combined. The people of Minnesota have multiplied as follows: 1850, 6,077; 1860, 172,023; 1870, 439,706; 1880, 770,773; 1890, 1,301,826.

Their assessed wealth has increased in this wise: 1860, $32,018,773; 1870, $84,135,332; 1880, $258,028,687; 1890, $588,531,745. The wealth of Minnesota has more than doubled in each decade of its existence, and in thirty years has multiplied nineteen fold.

During the past decade the population of the seven states tributary to Minneapolis increased 250 per cent., and their wealth 500 per cent. From a per capita valuation of less than $300 in 1880, the increase has reached nearly $500 per capita in 1890.

The latest Northwest enterprise is the development of the linen industry. Minnesota raised this year 466,000 acres in flax. The latest invention in flax machinery will take the ripe straw from which the seed has been threshed and produce from it a fiber equal to the best for manufacture into linen. This invention and the fertile soil of the Northwest will soon make linen, says Senator Pettigrew, as cheap as cotton. Minneapolis has extensive mills now in operation, and is giving to the world the first samples of Northwestern linens.

Miscellaneous Items.

A farmer near Garretson paid $100 for a lot of sheep a year ago. He has cleared $109.10 from them, and now has fifty-three head to pay for keeping.

Alexandria (Hanson county) Journal: C. M. Cooper brought to this office samples of rye and alfalfa. They are both of excellent growth. Mr. Cooper considers the alfalfa a paying crop and excellent food for stock.

Centerville (Turner County) Journal: H. E. Pelton tells of ten acres of oats near Hurley that threshed out 990 bushels, and as they will weigh out ten bushels to the hundred over machine measure, that will be considerably over 100 bushels per acre.

Dell Rapids (Minnehaha county) Times: The editor of a national paper called the American Investments, writes to the Times as follows:

"Will you please send me that copy of your paper which contains the report of the operations of twenty farmers in the big Sioux Valley? We are helping the restoration of confidence in the much abused West."

There is one farmer in Yankton county who offered his 160 acres of improved land a year ago for $7,000 and now he is glad he did not find a purchaser. His crops this year, calculated at ruling prices, will bring him $3,500, or one-half the value of the place. And he does not reckon his hogs, cattle or horses. His farm is located six miles from Yankton on the James River.

Julius Gunderson brought to this office yesterday some samples of apples raised on his farm, southeast of Vermillion. The Red Astrakan, strawberry and two varieties of crab-apples were good samples of what Clay county soil will produce in the way of fruit, and they would be a credit to any fruit-growing state. In talking of crops, Mr. Gunderson said he never raised such crops before. His wheat will go 30 bushels to the acre.

Vermillion (Clay county) Republican: Ab. Anderson, living in the bend southwest of Vermillion, does not hesitate to say that his corn will go 100 bushels to the acre and potatoes 400. In order to verify this statement, Mr. Anderson proposes to have the ground measured by the county surveyor, and affidavit to the amount given. The corn and potatoes will be carefully measured when gathered.

A good many sheep are being shipped to South Dakota this year. The grain crop in most parts of the state is abundant, but farmers are learning from experience that it is not wise to depend on that crop alone. The man who has a good flock of sheep on his farm, and takes care of them, is sure of something that he can turn into cash every year.

A farmer named Clute, living near Plankinton, brought in a beet to exhibit at the grain palace which measured 3 ft. 4 in. in length.

Yankton Press: South Dakota has credit in the general summaries of the wheat crop for 40,000,000 bushels. This quantity has been produced in forty different counties. The farmers will realize from it not less than 80c a bushel, which will amount to $32,000,000 for this one product. Wheat is not the leading cereal in South Dakota. Corn will excel it and the oat will crowd it very close. Taking them all together with barley, rye and live stock, and the result of this year's product will be found to equal at least the total assessed value of all property in the state for 1891.

Yankton Press: A land that produces 30 bushels of wheat, 80 bushels of oats, 75 of corn and 300 bushels of potatoes to the acre, is a land that will support a dense population. Such is South Dakota. The population will come speedily.

THE BLACK HILLS DISTRICT - 1890'S

John M. White presents an interesting general description of the Black Hills in discussing his tour of the area.

Source: John M. White. <u>The Newer Northwest</u>. St. Louis, Mo.: Self Culture Publishing Co., 1894, 28-64.

> "St. Mary! what a scene is here!
> I've traversed many a mountain-strand
> Abroad and in my native land,
> And it has been my lot to tread
> Where safety more than pleasure led;
> But by my halidome,
> A scene so wide, so wild as this,
> Yet so sublime in barrenness,
> Ne'er did my wandering footsteps press."
> —*Lord of the Isles.*

EDGEMONT lies at the gateway of the Black Hills. Here the road divides before the rocky barrier which opposes, and turning right and left makes its way to the recesses of two of the spurs of the Rocky mountains. The main road turning westward, rounds the southern end of the "Hills," and pursuing a northwest course, penetrates the Big Horn mountains, and thence reaches Billings, Montana. The "Hills" division follows the valley of the Cheyenne for three or four miles to the east, when it turns sharply north, and climbing close to the summit, traverses the whole length of this remarkable mountain region.

We reached Edgemont at seven o'clock and took breakfast at the "Burlington." The hostelry is typical of the railroad system whose name it bears. It is large, roomy, beautifully situated, superior in its appointments, and elegantly conducted. It has worthily earned the high reputation it bears among all experienced travelers. As we sat discussing the appetizing menu presented, Johnson proposed that we lie over one day, just to enjoy the hotel and study the country, and I gladly assented.

The region about Edgemont is a delightful agricultural country, destined to become the home of a dense and prosperous population. The surface is pleasantly diversified, the soil is deep, fertile, and possessed of enduring qualities that makes it a mine of wealth. The lack of a sufficient natural supply of water has retarded its settlement, but with irrigation, and the superb railroad system which brings a ready market right to the door of this section, it is bound to be rapidly filled with enterprising farmers. A large irrigating canal, designed to distribute the never-failing water of the Cheyenne throughout this region, is now in course of construction. The rapidly growing cities of the "Hills," as well as the great outlet toward the southeast, are certain to supply a demand for all the surplus product. Such considerations, combined with the delightful natural surroundings, need only to be understood to awaken the western fever in the already crowded precincts of the middle states, with all its early power.

But the Black Hills district, proper, is not devoid of agricultural endowments. Its early notoriety and its present prosperity are primarily due to its mineral deposits, and fully eighty-five per cent. of its population are engaged in mining pursuits; and yet, skirting the foot of this rocky upheaval are beautiful prairies watered by the sparkling streams that find their source in the hills. Here the soils have been found deep and exceedingly productive, and many who have been attracted by the glittering promise of the placers have turned aside to the more congenial labor and the not less reliable returns of the farm. In such environments, there is a zest in outdoor life, freed from the din and dirt, the rush and the risk of a mine, that gold cannot buy. It is barely three years since the railroad climbed these hills, and the mining interests have so entirely obscured all other resources hitherto, that the agricultural possibilities have been largely ignored. There is apparently no exception in the list of cereals and vegetables that can be grown with complete success.

Little attention has as yet been given to fruit culture. Experiments with a few hardy varieties of apples have been made here and there, with marked success. These have been made by farmers in the valleys at the foot of the hills for domestic purposes, but systematic efforts have been made by a nurseryman located on the eastern slope of the Hills. The results attained have been gratifying in a high degree. The yield of apples has proved unusually large, and the quality exceptionally good. The successful culture of small fruits has been demonstrated by the returns of several years, and strawberries, raspberies, blackberries and gooseberries, currants and grapes are found especially productive. The award of the Dakota State Fair for the size and quality of fruits exhibited, was bestowed upon a fruit-grower of the Black Hills.

The stock interests of this region have not been so much neglected. The natural advantages for stock-raising are not excelled anywhere. The rich grasses of the region afford an abundance of nutritious pasturage, and readily curing on the stem, provide an excellent substitute for hay. This dried grass is the staple of the winter pasturage which seldom fails on the south side of the hills, even in the severest weather. The protection afforded by the mountains and the general altitude combine to produce exceptional qualities in the native-bred horse of this region. His muscular development, lung power and endurance are noticeably superior to the similar features in animals bred elsewhere. This fact is becoming more widely recognized every year, and has given this interest a great impetus. It is estimated that there are now a hundred thousand head of horses on the ranches of this region.

SITTING BULL—BUFFALO BILL.

Cattle are extensively grown also. Roaming the ranges in all seasons without special care, and readily driven to distant railroad points, the business early sprang up and flourished here. Increased railroad facilities, and the development of nearer markets are certain to stimulate an already profitable enterprise. An annual product of sixty thousand head, with a value of some two millions of dollars, is the present estimate of the cattle business.

Sheep need more care, and have not been raised here in any large way. There are some successful and profitable flocks of good size, and there seems to be a notable absence of those diseases which prove such obstacles to successful wool growing elsewhere. It would seem that this industry could be profitably enlarged.

All this, and much more, I learned from certain guests of the hotel who seemed to be loaded for just such game as I proved to be. The array of statistics submitted in support of these statements was appalling to a fellow not up in figures, and if they are rather tamely put, it is due to my inability to grasp the immense mass of fact and illustration which my innocent inquiries brought out. In this way we spent the day, visiting in the meantime the railroad repair-shops established here, and other points of interest. After dinner we sat upon the broad porch. Before us stretched the wide expanse of green to the river's edge, with the railroad crossing the space between. To the left, portentious in the deepening shadows, towered the huge pile of rocks I had come so far to see. Its slopes were hidden by a forest of pine and hemlock, the deep green of which appears so dark in the distance as to suggest the distinctive name which these hills bear.

"As the evening shades prevail," we fall into the mood of the hour, and sit silent, inhaling the balsamic odors of the pines as they mingle with the rising incense of our cigars in the dewy air. At length, Johnson breaks the silence.

"I say, John, I'm not given to sentimentalism, but I'll be hanged if it don't seem pretty hard lines to lose such a glorious country as this after an undisturbed possession for two hundred years, and no one knows how much longer. The trouble with the Indian is, that he isn't practical. He ought to have put a wire fence about these prairies and raised buffaloes for the market. Later he could have laid off the "bad lands" into town lots and advertised the buttes as vineyard sites. If he won half the success the land jobbers did in Illinois just before the panic of 1837, he could have retired to his pipe of peace on a cheerful competence, and hired a cheap hand to hunt his breakfast for him in the morning.

"The Dakotas were a brave race, as Indians go, and were to this western country what the Iroquois were to the Atlantic border. They held their own, and something more, until they came in contact with the white man's firearms and fire-water. The Algonkin tribes called them "Nadowessioux," which the early French explorers of Canada shortened into Sioux. When the whites first learned of them in 1640, they occupied the vast region extending from Devil's lake to the Missouri river, and extending westward to the main range of the Rocky mountains. For two centuries they maintained the lines of this empire unbroken, but in 1837, they ceded away all their lands east of the Mississippi, and since then they have waged a losing contest. In 1851, they fell back to a line drawn from Otter Tail Lake, through Lake Traverse to the junction of the Big Sioux with the Missouri, retaining out of the ceded territory, however, a tract twenty by a hundred and forty miles. This cession was made reluctantly, and as the general government grossly neglected the provisions of the treaty, bad feeling was early engendered and it needed only a fit opportunity to precipitate open hostilities.

"This came in 1854, when Lieutenant Grattan, attempting to arrest an Indian, attacked a village and was cut off with his whole party. Of course, war followed with the usual atrocities until the savages were defeated at Little Blue Water, in the fall of 1855, by General Harney. An armed neutrality rather than a peace succeeded, and in the summer of 1857, the bloody Sioux announced the beginning of a new campaign by the massacre of forty-seven settlers near Spirit lake. Another signal defeat resulted in another treaty, by which the eastern limit of the Sioux empire was fixed at the line of the Missouri river. In 1862, Little Crow's band assumed the offensive, made a marauding expedition into Minnesota, butchered the settlers at Breckenridge, and then made two vigorous assaults on Fort Abercrombie, across the river. In the latter attacks they were repulsed with heavy loss, and were subsequently pursued to Wood's lake where they were brought to bay and badly worsted. About a thousand whites lost their lives in the Indian war of 1862-63, while besides suffering the usual casualties some of the most troublesome tribes were driven into the British possessions, and a thousand made prisoners. Thirty-nine of these were subsequently tried and hung for their outrages.

"In the meantime, the war of the rebellion intervened. Little notice was taken of the desultory hostilities maintained by the savages, the operations of the frontier forces being confined to preserving the *statu quo*. General Harney had penetrated this region in 1855, and given his name to its loftiest peak, and in the following year General Warren had pushed his explorations as far as Inyan Kara, when he was compelled to retire to avoid open hostilities. Fort Phil Kearney was subsequently established near a spur of the Big Horn mountains, and in 1866 was the object of a spirited attack, while a wood-train with a strong military guard under the command of Colonel Fetterman was entirely cut off, almost in sight of the fort. A campaign and the military guards in September, the squatters returned, re-located the city, and in five months numbered seven thousand. In this time fifteen hundred structures had been erected—rude

SIOUX—BEFORE AND AFTER.

affairs constructed of pine logs with a roof of dirt, but affording ample shelter for domestic and business purposes. In the same period, ninety places of trade, exclusive of saloons, had opened for business. Hill City, sixteen miles north, was only a few weeks later in the race, but the discovery of the rich placer of Deadwood, in the spring of 1876, created a stampede in that direction that resembled nothing so well as the mad rush of a frightened herd on the plains. In three weeks Hill City was as deserted as a graveyard, and Custer had by actual count just fourteen men left.

"Then followed a period of delirious excitement. Each new 'find' gave rise to exaggerated stories of its richness, and as the story traveled, it gained in every proportion and quality save in respect of veracity. Men became unsettled, and absolutely impoverished in the midst of the very gold they craved. The land speculator, profiting by the general craze, platted cities right and left, and operated on a scale that would have done credit to a city of the first class. In many cases the span of urban life was very brief, but in the fall of 1877, nineteen towns and mining camps were represented in a convention held at that date. The population was then estimated at ten to fifteen thousand. This was by no means the highest point reached, but the sifting process had begun. A large part of the "driftwood" had been eliminated. It was still, however, a frontier mining community, with all that that implies, but in it all could be seen the chaos of a mighty world rounding into form.'

"Well, the easy placer mines soon became exhausted. The quartz mines were discovered, and systematic mining became necessary everywhere. This involved the investment of capital, and the protection only afforded by social stability. In 1886, the tedious and insecure stage routes were superceded by the railway. In 1890, the Indian reservation which intervened between the Black Hills and the Missouri river was thrown open to settlers, and in the following year the rich trade current of this wonderful region ran pulsating through the commercial arteries of the Burlington system to all the great centers of the world.

"Before undertaking the costly and difficult enterprise of building an extension of its line through the heart of the Hills, north and south, the Burlington management thoroughly sounded the resources of the region through a distinguished expert, who spent two years in his researches. The result may be summed up in a phrase you have often heard, 'that the hundred miles square, comprising the Black Hills, is the richest spot of equal area now known on earth.' Gold is found in the Archaean area, from Bear gulch in the north to Point of Rocks in the south. Silver mining is yet in its infancy here. The presence of the metal in paying quantities has been demonstrated in the Carbonate and Galena districts of Lawrence county, and in one or two other localities. Tin is found in two well-defined belts, the "Nigger Hill" district, in Lawrence county and extending beyond its western border, covering an area of about four by six miles, and containing about four hundred mine locations; and the Harney district in Pennington county, forming a crescent about Harney Peak, with Hayward and Warren's gulch at the east and west points, respectively. There are about seven thousand locations in this district. It has long been the deliberate judgment of unbiased and competent experts, that there is an immense body of valuable tin ore in these hills, and the elaborate experiment made at Hill City has demonstrated the truth of these estimates.

"But the value of these mineral deposits is greatly enhanced by the fact that an immense deposit of first-class fuel lies right beside them. It is estimated that there are twelve thousand square miles of coal lands in this region. A belt of bituminous coking coal extends nearly the whole distance around the Hills, and is extensively mined at Cambria, on the western slope. Beside all this, copper, nickel, mica, gypsum, marble, onyx and endless quantities and varieties of building materials have been found, and developed sufficiently to demonstrate their commercial value. Lying up there between the forks of the Cheyenne, is a mass of assorted minerals, a hundred miles long, and from forty to sixty miles wide, that is destined to be a source of national wealth to the end of the world. More than fifty thousand mining claims have been located under the United States laws, and only a few hundred of them have been practically developed.

"The wealth of this country is a prodigious fact," he said in closing, and I was too far overwhelmed to reply. It was late in the night; our cigars were long since exhausted, and I left my companion nervously chewing the unconsumed end of his "La Tosca," too absorbed in the story he had been telling to notice my "good night." I went to bed and to sleep, but for hours I seemed conscious of a mental undertone which fell into the rythm of Miss Killmansegg's moral:

"Gold! Gold! Gold! Gold!
Bright and yellow, hard and cold.
* * * * * *
How widely its agencies vary—
To save—to ruin—to curse—to bless—
As even its minted coins express,
Now stamped with the image of Good Queen Bess,
And now of a Bloody Mary."

> "Here in the sultriest season let him rest,
> Fresh is the green beneath those aged trees;
> Here winds of gentlest wing will fan his breast,
> From heaven itself he may inhale the breeze;
> The plain is far beneath. Oh! let him seize
> Pure pleasure while he can; the scorching ray
> Here pierceth not, impregnate with disease;
> Then let his length the loitering pilgrim lay,
> And gaze, untired, the morn, the noon, the eve away."
> —*Childe Harold's Pilgrimage.*

BRIGHT and early the next morning we board the train for the valley of Minnekahta. The road follows the general trend of Sheep canyon, for ten or twelve miles, when it crosses the great chasm just before reaching our destination. This canyon is a deep cleft in the foot-hills, taking its origin some thirty miles north of the Cheyenne. Its initial course is a little west of south until it reaches the vicinity of Minnekahta, where taking a semi-circular sweep about this point, it comes back to the east side of the railroad and ends near Edgemont. The great fissure deepens as it proceeds, until it reaches a depth of four hundred feet. The road crosses it just below and above Minnekahta, affording on either hand a view of its awful sides, clothed from top to bottom by a sturdy growth of conifers.

Minnekahta is the junction where the visitor to Hot Springs transfers himself and traps to a waiting train, which carries him on a winding trail among the lesser hills, and in thirty-five minutes lands him in the "Carlsbad of America." The site of the junction alone bears the attractive appellation which in the Sioux tongue characterizes the thermal quality of the waters of this region. It once had a wider application, but the practical demand for a plainer term substituted the less euphonious name of Hot Springs for the town. We follow the course of the Fall river valley winding in and out among the lesser hills until we emerge from the labyrinth, and glide along the banks of Hotbrook into the center of the town. We are still amid the encircling hills, but here, on either side, solid structures of storied sandstone greet the stranger's wondering gaze, and proclaim a prosperous and cultivated civilization for which the approach has afforded little preparation. I dumbly follow my companion, as the train ceases its motion, and soon find myself settled at the Evans Hotel, a five-story, stone castellated pile, with mosaic-floored lobby, frescoed walls, electroliers and modern luxury in all its appointments. It is a vision of Saratoga let down in the Black Hills.

The formality of introductions, unpacking and toilet attentions bring us to the dinner hour, and thus fairly adjusted to our new environment, we seat ourselves on the broad veranda which extends its four hundred feet of length about three sides of the building, and take in the situation while we enjoy an after-dinner cigar. Scarcely a stone's throw away from where we sit, the brook gurgles by, a clear, active, sparkling stream, disclosing in its every characteristic, its free mountain birth. Following the curve of a narrow valley, it lies before us a bow of silver, while the light bridge, which spans its shores in front of us, marks the roadway that, like an arrow, speeds its flashing course toward the western hills until lost 'mid the deep green of its verdure. Midway of the ascent, within its own generous domain of nature, softened by the hand of art, the Soldiers' Home rears its stately pile. To the left, in the near distance, half hidden by private residences and trees, stands the Black Hills College. In the foreground across the brook, is the "Gillespie," a four-storied hotel in pink sandstone, with a two-storied veranda, like flounces, along its double front, and a corner tower which commands a fine view of the entire valley. North of the "Gilles-

The railroad is its principal thoroughfare, and the throngs which it brings dominate the institutions of the place. Though less than five years old, and with a population of less than three thousand, its precocious urbanity strikes none with so little surprise as itself. It began life with a profound and abiding faith in its own high destiny, and accepts its growing success as its birthright. The one fair daughter among many wealthy and powerful brothers in the Hills, it expected to be sought out and flattered, and is not surprised at the event. But with all this assurance, it does not fail to be gracious. No pains are spared to please its guests, and its standard of excellence is the world's best.

The springs are very much *en evidence* everywhere. The natives were the original discoverers, and are said to have tested the curative qualities of the waters with the most satisfactory results, for, to paraphrase a well-known doggerel,

> The native when sick, in hot water will lave;
> The native when well, devil a bit will he have.

The curious are shown on Battle mountain the evidences of its former occupation by a numerous Indian population, and a legend is told the visitor of a famous fight which took place on this hill for the possession of these delectable mountains. The narrator will insist that the springs were the bone of contention, but waiving such trivial considerations, the story with proper embellishments affords a romantic background for modern history. The Cheyennes, it is said were established here some fifty years ago, when the Sioux, having a solicitous regard for the health of the women and children, ousted the tenants at will *vi et armis*.

The original spring, the head and front of the town's existence, is found at the northern end of the valley. The early facilities for bathing were very inadequate, and writers have waxed pathetic in describing how the afflicted savage immersed himself by sections until he bethought himself to set the squaws to enlarging the natural basin. But there is no scarcity of the water which pours its tepid stream through the center of the town, and if there be anything sure in this uncertain world, its medicinal character is not elsewhere equaled. It has been repeatedly analyzed and the results of the analysis by Profesor G. A. Maviner, of Chicago, have been abundantly confirmed. His finding is expressed as follows:

Constituents per gallon.	Grains.
Silica	2.464
Peroxide of iron	a trace
Calcium sulphate	16.325
Magnesium sulphate	4.320
Sodium sulphate, Potassium sulphate }	25.620
Sodium chloride and potassa	13.790
Total	62.519

To this may be added the recommendation of reputable physicians, of which hundreds have visited this place to satisfy themselves by personal examination of the exact facts in the case. They say:

From observation and information we recommend Hot Springs as one of the best resorts for those suffering from rheumatism, gout, constitutional syphilis, malarial fever, chronic malarial poisoning, most chronic diseases of the liver, kidneys and bladder, chronic bronchitis and bronchial asthma, incipient consumption, all varieties of indigestion and catarrh of the stomach, hysteria, neurasthemia, neuralgia and chronic skin diseases.

We love you for your charming scenery, your pure air and limpid waters; your bright and genial clime, giving to all perfect health and complete rest. We will come again and send our friends.

ROBERT D. BRADLEY, M. D., Peoria, Ill.
GEO. F. JENKINS, M. D., Keokuk, Ia., Pres. Keokuk Medical School.
M. N. McNAUGHTON, M. D., Villisca, Ia.
F. M. HIETT, M. D., Red Oak, Ia.
Committee.

This is all very well for the profession, but what to an unprofessional observer is far stronger evidence, is afforded by the experiment of the Board of Managers of the National Home for Dependent Veterans. The availability of Hot Springs for the location of a national hospital had come to the board's attention, and in July, 1893, a detail of thirty invalids was sent here. The condition of each individual of the detail was minutely noted, and at the end of sixty days the results were summed up by the surgeon in charge, as follows:

The number of men sent was thirty; time given for the test, sixty days; age of youngest, 46 years; age of oldest, 71 years; average age, 52 years. As it will be observed from the above report, the cases of locomotor ataxia, arthritis deformans and aberration of mind conceded to be incurables, and sent only with the hope that some alleviation of suffering might be obtained, as well as others on account of advanced age, broken constitutions and a complication of diseases, makes this an exceedingly severe test, and contrary to expectations, cures have been effected and permanent benefit secured. Almost every man was afflicted with rheumatism and nervous trouble, the same being cured in every instance. I am satisfied that a careful inspection by the Medical Board will bear me out in the assertion that all things considered, age of patients, their shattered constitutions, variety and complications of diseases, and the chronic nature of all, that the result of this test, as shown by the detailed report, is in every sense highly satisfactory. A realization of all the claims put forth by the promoters of this experiment as to the virtues of the waters and climate of Hot Springs, South Dakota, and its desirability for the location of a United States Sanitarium for the treatment of such chronic diseases as most affect the old soldiers, have been fulfilled.

Nothing can be added to such evidence save personal experience. The visitor hears of well authenticated cures of rheumatism; acute, inflammatory and sciatica; diseases resulting from the use of mercury; neuralgia of the head, face, stomach or limbs; catarrh; ascites or dropsy; hemorrhoids or piles; dyspepsia or chronic indigestion; constipation; nephritis and other diseases of the kidneys; urinary difficulties; eczema, psoriasis and all other diseases of the skin; while female complaints of various characters; diseases of the stomach and alimentary canal; liver complaint, and bright's disease of the kidneys, are very much relieved and sometimes cured. The temperature is a feature of these waters very much emphasized It is about ninety-eight degrees Fahrenheit, so close to the temperature of the human body as to require neither heating nor cooling to suit it to bathing purposes, and it is asserted that at this point liquids absorb and retain the largest percentage of gaseous and volatile matters. At high temperature, these valuable properties are expelled, leaving only the less efficient to act upon the sytem.

The waters are agreeable to the taste and may be freely drank with the happiest results. They cleanse the stomach, stimulate the secretion of the glandular system, augment the change of tissue, allay muscular irritability, and make one at peace with himself and the world. The drinking fountain of the Evans Hotel is supplied from the Minnekahta spring, and right across the brook from the hotel is the Hygeia,

> "A marble-paved pavilion, where a spring
> Of living water from the center flows,
> Whose bubbling does a genial freshness fling."

Add to this a climate that is a delightful marvel to the most experienced, and you possess a natural sanitarium not elsewhere equaled. Every favorable condition seems to have combined to take this valley out of the jurisdiction of the weather bureau. Its altitude touches the golden mean between the seaboard and those higher levels, that prove so exacting to the strongest. It stands thirty-seven hundred feet above the ocean level, and many afflicted with hay-fever, asthma, bronchitis and pulmonary ailments, who find the Colorado altitude too severe, come here and find relief. Variations of temperature are characterized by the same moderation. The fierce extremes of summer and winter are unknown. The average temperature of the winter months is forty-two degrees Fahrenheit, above zero, and a variation of fifty degrees will cover the annual range of the mercury. These favorable conditions are apparently confined to a limited area, as within the radius of ten miles there is a difference of ten or fifteen degrees in the thermometrical markings. The seasons blend rather than change, and the summer reigns the unchallenged sovereign of the rolling year. The annual precipitation is light, probably not exceeding twenty inches, and there are more days of sunshine here than anywhere else outside of a fairy story. According to the official records of the signal service, the average year has 88 cloudy, 167 partly cloudy and 110 (in leap years 111) perfectly clear days.

These conditions probably owe their origin to the peculiar situation of the locality and to the numerous springs of hot water found here. A general view of the Hot Springs valley reveals a broad sweep of undulating hills between two lofty ranges, which run in a general north and south direction. Outlined by fringes of evergreen timber are numerous gulches, meandering in all directions and dividing the lesser hills into island groups. These act as air chambers in which the breeze, cooled by the mountain-fed streams, freely circulates with its burden of aromatic fragrance. Cyclones and blizzards are only phantoms of the meteorologist's brain to this sequestered spot. Storms which touch the loftier hills wreak their strength against these invincible guardians of the valley below, and their broken fragments are borne across the guarded space on the air current which sets from west to east.

Predestination finds no stronger bulwark for its doctrine than in the conditions which have been so imperfectly noted, and sanitariums have risen here as naturally as the evergreen forests on the hillsides. There are numberless springs throughout this gulch, but the principal ones are the Minnekahta, the Mammoth, Lakota and the Catholicon. These have all been analyzed with substantially the same results as noted on a previous page. Over the Minnekahta is a two-storied bath-house containing some sixty bathing apartments. These are heated by steam, handsomely floored with mottled tiles and equipped with marble tubs of modern design. The attendance and accessories are all that could be wished. Situated in a retired niche of the hills, this establishment affords a delightful sense of seclusion that none can so well appreciate as the convalescent. Here a moccasin-shaped tub, carved out of solid rock, is shown as the one originally used by the natives. A four-story sanitarium, fitted to please the taste and convenience of the guest, is conducted in connection with the bath-house, and is situated near by.

But for those who retain a zest for the robust pleasures of life, the "Plunge" will probably offer the greatest attraction. This is a magnificent idea, superbly wrought in stone, wood, iron and glass. A basin, fifty by two hundred and fifty feet, with cement sides and a gravel bottom from which rise a thousand bubbling springs, is fed by the mammoth spring which pours a flood of a hundred thousand gallons of water per hour. The outpour maintains a bathing depth of from four feet at one end to nine feet at the other. A wide open gallery surrounds it, affording ample space for bathers and spectators. Here at convenient points are provided toboggan slides, trapeze, spring-boards, floats, ropes and every device that experience in water sports can suggest. It is a pleasure resort, and the most delightful place to learn to swim, if one be so minded. But notwithstanding all of this profusion, it is not the ordinary H. 2 O. chemical formula for water that is provided. The water, so agreeable to the touch, is heated in nature's kitchen, and is charged with chemicals that renew one's strength like the eagle's. It is highly impregnated with magnetic properties which are distinctly observable, and is so clear that the pebbles at the bottom may be distinctly seen by one from the margin of the pool. Aside from the mere joy of bathing, therefore, those of us on the shady side of life, who feel the twinges of rheumatism without caring to own it, find it admirably adapted to what ails us, and—" Tell it not in Gath, lest the daughters of the Philistines rejoice,"—my dear, it has a magical effect in removing freckles, moth and wrinkles. Over all is a unique structure with arched roof, heated by steam, lighted by electricity and provided with a hundred dressing-rooms where every accessory of a well appointed city establishment may be found.

Adjoining the "Evans" is a three-story sanitarium, built of cut sandstone similar to that of the hotel. In outward design it corresponds to the castellated style of the larger structure, and in finish and furnishings is completed with the same elegance. It is heated with steam and lighted with electricity. Handsomely furnished offices and waiting-rooms are found on the ground floor, and apartments for sixty occupants in the other stories. The rooms are *en suite* so that the invalid may be served at the least expenditure of strength. The sanitarium is separate from the hotel, though connected by an enclosed passageway, and each apartment has an outside exposure. The bathing pools are roomy and fitted with variegated tiles. It is designed for the convenience not only of the guests of the hotel but also for the general public. Every form of bath conducive to health may be had here, including the Carlsbad, Turkish, vapor, silver, needle, medicated and mud bath. The attendance is under the direction of competent physicians, and every facility to be found anywhere is provided.

Doctor A. S. Stewart has established a sanitarium and bath-house on the western slope, with accommodations for twenty-two patients. Facilities for hot or cold baths, Turkish, vapor and spray are provided. The rooms are arranged with a professional care of the wants of the invalid. The interior finish is in oiled white pine; the rooms are large and airy, provided with large windows that give access to the genial sunshine, so important in cases of ill health. The bath-rooms are furnished with elaborate marble tubs, and floored with colored tiling in attractive designs. A unique feature of this private establishment is its plunge-bath in the center of the building. It is twenty-five feet in diameter, and may be supplied with water at any desirable temperature or to any required depth. The waters have the same medicinal qualities as the other springs, and afford a privacy for small parties that can be secured nowhere else so well. Board and lodging may be secured at cottages near by, if desired, and patrons are assured of the attendance of a competent physician at all times.

The Catholicon sanitarium, situated on the slopes overlooking the newer part of the town, is an imposing structure, seventy-five by one hundred feet, built of pressed brick and native stone. The patronage of this spring has been very liberal, compelling several additions to the original structure. The sanitarium has a capacity for the accommodation of forty guests, but when the newer structure is opened, it will offer ninety more rooms to the public.

The Sulphur spring is the outflow of an artesian well a hundred and eighty feet deep. The bath-house erected here is in a delightfully romantic region, and is one of the charming spots that every visitor should see. All told, a thousand persons may be accommodated in the different sanitariums and enjoy the vigorating stimulus that these remarkable waters afford. But this is only a beginning of the patronage that those best informed expect, and plans are forming to greatly increase the present facilities at no distant date. And there is no reason to question these sanguine expectations. Not only are the curative qualities of the waters unquestioned, but the scenery still bears the mark of nature's hand unspoiled by the littleness of art. The traveling facilities afforded by the " Burlington " transfer the visitor without unpleasant sense of change, and one leaves the comforts of the modern city only to find them perfectly installed in this cleft of the mountains, with all that a cultivated taste can add to make them all one's own.

> "Now the soft hour
> Of walking comes; for him who lonely loves.
> To seek the distant hills, and there converse
> With nature; there to harmonize his heart,
> And in pathetic song to breathe around
> The harmony to others."
>
> —*Thomson.*

THE atmosphere of Hot Springs is full of the zest of living. Here and there the drawn features of disease claim the attention, but the throngs which populate its hotels and people its streets, are here for the recuperation to be found in its aromatic air, in the untrammeled freedom of its landscapes, and in the stimulus of its mountain rambles and invigorating waters. The regular hotel menu has no suggestion of the dyspeptic's diet. Doubtless the delicate appetite of the invalid is consulted in the proper place, but the *table d'hote* anticipates the robust relish born of mountain breeze and exercise.

Electricity and the modern express service have annihilated time and space. Spread before us, with all the elegant accessories of refinement, were the choice spoils of the globe, from the tropics to the poles, with the dew of freshness still upon them. The hackneyed phrase of the shop is here inverted, and if the most fickle taste goes unsatisfied it is because the resources of nature and the chef's art are exhausted, and there is nothing more to seek.

It was with this sense of complete satisfaction that my companion and I took our seats in a retired part of the great veranda at the close of our first day's stay in the hills. The lengthening shadows of the twilight hour softened the bold outlines of the day, and here and there the electric twinkle seemed to reflect the starry lights of the calm, blue sky above us. The hush of the evening fell on all animate nature, and save the indistinct hum of the human hive behind us and the far-off murmur of the street, there was nothing to obtrude the environments of existence upon us. The strife of living seemed to die out and leave only the sensuous seeming of a dream. The delight of such an hour is to exquisite for words.

"'Tis lone,
And wonderful, and deep, and hath a sound
And sense, and sight of sweetness,"

unknown to the exactions of life's realities.

How long we sat, loth to break the enchanting spell with words, or whether our soaring spirits would ever have returned to their tenements of clay without outside assistance are unsolved problems. We had become dimly conscious of the lilting melody of the waltz, and broken sounds of an increased animation in the circle just beyond our horizon, had come to us on the wings of the winds that gently fanned the place, when we were brought in contact with sublunary things by the cordial greeting of a friend of my companion.

"Why, Johnson," he exclaimed, "I did not know you were here. Permit me to present you to our friend, Miss H——, of Boston. You will recognize Mrs. B——, I'm sure. She ignores the demands of time and leaves me to pay the tribute of age for us both. We were in quest of just such a quiet nook, and if you will permit we'll intrude on your reverie for a quiet moment or two."

"E'en in our ashes live their wonted fires," and it was not difficult to believe that there was some vital relation between our dreams and the vision of fair women thus presented. We were soon comfortably adjusted to our new surroundings and afloat on the buoyant tide of cheerful talk.

"Is this your first visit to Hot Springs, Mr. Johnson?" inquired Miss H——.

"No," responded my companion, "but I am here at present rather in the capacity of a guide to my friend, White, who made his debut this morning."

"O, you have many a delight in store," she replied, turning to me. This is my first visit, but I have been here several weeks, and each day discloses some new charm in this sequestered spot. Mamma and I spend the heated term in some cool retreat every year, and we have heard so much of Hot Springs from our friends here that we determined to try it this year, but mamma's courage failed at the last moment and she went off to the old places, and I am here without her. I know she'll regret her decision when I tell her of this charming country. But I am by no means alone in my discovery. I have met friends from Chicago here, and several persons from Providence, Cincinnati, Louisville, St. Louis and Omaha. I congratulate myself on the good judgment I have displayed, and quite envy Mrs. B——'s lot of living here the year round."

"Yes," responded Mrs. B——, "it is a place of infinite variety. Its beauty never stales; it is new every morning and fresh every evening."

"It is just the place for papa," interjected the vivacious Miss H——. "I am sure I shall be able to persuade him to come with me next year. You know how much he dislikes the fuss and feathers of the dress parade resorts; and that plunge is as good as the seaside for bathing. It is the one thing he grows enthusiastic over—the swimming, and the hills, and hunting of his boyhood days. It is so delightfully unconventional here that one feels as free as at home."

"Yes," chimed in our friend B——, "Hot Springs has proved a wonderful success in every way. I became interested here almost at the start, and the town has sprung into existence as if by magic. You will not find elsewhere as fine buildings and as elegant accommodations in any other town of five years' growth. Capital saw the natural advantages of this place at the first glance, and it has practically been a race for the first choice of investments. There are a dozen hotels, with an aggregate capacity of about a thousand guests. Besides these there are cottages and the sanitariums, which will accommodate about as many more. These are all so well filled that there are one or two projects now on foot to build more."

"O, well, added Johnson, one need not stay away for the lack of accommodations. For gentlemen, not accompanied by ladies, there is no more delightful way to spend a vacation than in camping out. I saw a most complete outfit for that purpose to-day, and the rental for the season was a trifling sum. There are a good many that spend the entire season under tents. The outfits to be had here are made up by experts, and besides saving the trouble of bringing it, one does not suffer the inconvenience of some oversight in making it up at home. In this way one can move from one location to another, as fancy suggests, and live like an uncrowned king in the enjoyment of life without its burdens."

And so the "current of unguided talk" ran on until our friends took their leave. With them went the incentive of the hour, and wearied with the experiences of the day we retired to a dreamless sleep that a farmer's lad might have envied.

We were out early in the morning, for as Johnson said, as he thundered at my door, the early hours are too glorious to be wasted in sleep. At early breakfast my companion explained the day's campaign. "We cannot stay here the whole season on the limit you have fixed," he said, "and we must take in a few of the principal features and get away. We can't see everything. Every peak has its particular landscape, and every one is well worth the trouble of getting to the coign of vantage to see. We'll go down to Cascade Springs this morning, and after a little rest for letters and cigars, we'll make up a party for the river drive."

To hear was to assent, and we were soon on the way toward the ambitious resort some nine or ten miles south of Hot Springs. It was an ideal morning. The unclouded blue of the sky reflected the glowing brightness of the sun through a filmy curtain of almost imperceptible haze, flooding every nook and corner of hill and dale with golden light. The road follows the old stage route to Denver and Cheyenne, over undulating hills and through shaded coves. Here and there the red or white gypsum rose in picturesque mounds or pillared forms, or towering in massive piles, turned their pictured walls in radiant greeting to the advancing sun. Over all was the dewy freshness of the morning, untouched by the sear and soil of exhausted nature. The air, charged with the odor of pine and hemlock, was full of the vigor of life, and it actually seemed extravagant to breathe it with unstinted enjoyment.

"BAD LANDS," NEAR HOT SPRINGS.

Some three or four miles out we stopped to examine the "Two Lone Wells," a *lusus naturæ*, notable even in this region of surprises. On the surface they appear simply two holes in the ground, ten or twelve feet in diameter, disclosing depths estimated at one or two hundred feet. It is explained that these dimensions are for the assurance of the timid ; that, in fact, the bottom has fallen out and left these wells dry in a land abounding with springs. It is suggested that there is no scientific reason why they may not ultimately afford a short route for the Celestials, who will certainly want to visit this wonderful region.

The day was still in its early hours when we reached Cascade Springs. The little town is situated in a picturesque valley, surrounded by high hills, whose slopes are clothed with the resinous pine. A number of springs bubble out of the ground here with an ample flow of cool water, highly charged with medicinal minerals. Some three years ago a syndicate purchased a large tract, including the springs, platted it, and laid the foundation of a health resort. A costly sanitarium and spacious dancing pavilion are the chief features of the place. It is an attractive point for picnic parties from Hot Springs, who bring their luncheon and music and spend the day in dancing, bathing and rambling, as fancy favors. Below the town is the Cascade, where the overflow of the springs dashes down the shelving rocks, charming the spectator with the prismatic beauty of its spray and the sprightly plunge of its noisy torrent.

Our return was made in good time for the midday meal, and after discussing our letters, a dozing hour made us again "fit for stratagems and spoils." In the meantime the restless Johnson had provided a capacious vehicle, invited our friends of the previous evening, and at three o'clock we started out for a drive along Fall river. The stream makes its way to the Cheyenne through the rocky barriers that encircle the site of Hot Springs, leaving but scant room for the wheelway which presses close to its margin for four or five miles. The drive follows an old stage route, rich with the legends of the days before the advent of railroads. A tall cliff which dominates a narrow pass, where the road makes a sharp curve about a point of rocks, is pointed out as the watch tower, from which the approaching stage, with its golden load, was descried, and the signal passed to the lurking highwaymen below.

The road rounds the base of Battle mountain, whose precipitous sides seem to defy all approach to its lofty summit. It is readily reached, however, from another direction, and as its stupendous bulk seemed about to block our pathway, Mrs. B—— inquired: "Have you seen the outlook from the summit yet, Mr. White?" As I replied in the negative, she responded: "O, you must not miss that. It is a glorious sight. As far as the eye can reach on every side rise individual peaks, with great mountain masses stretching miles and miles beyond. It is like a council of leaders in the midst of opposing armies, and suggests an encounter of the gods such as Homer loved to picture. On ordinary occasions one can discover familiar localities sixty-five miles away. But the sunrise is its crowning sight. As the first rays of the sun touch the lofty summits of the hills, peak after peak lights up its great beacon-fire until the whole mountain mass is ablaze with the sun's glory. Below, the mists slowly rise, disclosing valley, canyon and cove, dotted here and there with drowsy herds, the scattered farmhouses and the clustered homes of the villages. It is magnificent, but indescribable."

The drive is marked by parti-colored rocks, attractive landscapes and odorous groves of evergreens, but its climacteric feature is the falls of Minnekahta. This is a beautiful cascade, the river dashing over and around great blocks of red sandstone, blending its rainbow hues with the deeper coloring of its rocky channel. It is a memory that one will not willingly let die.

Late that evening Johnson greeted me with the announcement: "I've arranged a distinguished honor as well as a new surprise for you. My friend Sidey has promised to take us out to the newly-discovered Onyx Cave to-morrow, and we shall be the first visitors that have been permitted to explore it."

"I am proof against all surprises in this country," I replied. "I am prepared to start for the moon at a moment's notice, and after mountains of gold and caves of onyx, I shall expect to find diamonds clinging to the roots of weeds. My only surprise is that people eat the ordinary potato is this country. If the cook should declare that they were thousand-dollar tulip bulbs, I should place implicit faith in his statement."

Early the next morning a superb span of bays attached to an easy spring wagon stood before the door, and dispatching a hasty breakfast we got into our places and were soon in rapid motion up the valley. Before reaching the northern limit the road turns toward the eastern hills, and then northward again, up a charming canyon and on along the road that leads to Deadwood. The route we followed was marked by the beauties that everywhere characterize this region. Fine specimens of pine, spruce and hemlock cast their grateful shade athwart the way, while picturesque rocks, in mountain masses or in isolated forms, painted their variegated hues on the dark background of olive green. Here and there the undulations of the hills disclosed landscapes that exhausted the vocabulary of delight and dazed the sense, no longer able to grasp the grandeur of the panorama that passed before our eyes.

Some three or four miles out we stopped at a wayside spring to refresh man and beast with a draft of the cool, crystal-like fluid which flowed from a great fountain three or four feet in diameter. It was shaded by a single specimen of the rock spruce, a living obelisk of green, tapering up to a height of a hundred feet. This tree is a native of the mountain and is seldom found on the lower levels save when transplanted. It grows on the steepest slope, in the thinnest layers of soil, and not unfrequently thrusts its way through the solid stone. It seems to thrive on the scantiest nourishment, and when transplanted in rocky soil grows well in the valleys. A tree of several inches diameter is readily pulled up by hand.

Soon after leaving the spring a newly-made road branches to the left, and climbing a rather difficult hill, we reach a high plateau, over which we traveled for a mile or two until coming to a brook in the bottom of a canyon, we trace its upward course a half mile to the cave. The entrance was an insignificant opening, but nothing daunted we alighted and awaited the denouement. Having first divested ourselves of our outer clothing and donned some cast-off garments which our host had provided, we turned our backs upon the world and plunged into the dark recesses of the cave.

A spiral descent of four hundred feet, walled with onyx in layers of every hue, brought us to the first floor, where succeeding chambers opening into each other lead to a great wall of the precious mineral. An opening at the bottom invited the slim and daring to still farther recesses. Here we left our host, whose robust physique forbade his attempting the pass. An abject crawl of fifty feet through mud and water brought us to a small ante-room, from whence a slide of twenty feet introduced us into a beautiful chamber resplendant with the prismatic glories of the rainbow. Again a spiral descent of about eight hundred feet leads to an ante-chamber of moderate dimensions. A less difficult crawl of six or eight feet admits to a grand chamber or waiting-room, whence one descends a hundred and fifty feet to the grand audience-chamber, with a floor surface of about two acres. The vaulted ceiling towered beyond the reach of our candles, but the nearer surfaces reflected our light with such brilliancy that one easily imagined himself in the throne-room of the gnomes. Passages led to other unexplored recesses, but our curiosity was satisfied, and we retraced our way to the upper air.

* * *

AMONG THE BLACK HILLS - EARLY 20TH CENTURY

Clifton Johnson presents some aspects of the history, traditions, customs and personnell of South Dakota.

Source: Clifton Johnson. <u>Highways and Byways of the Rocky Mountains</u>. New York: The Macmillan Company, 1910, 250-263.

AMONG THE BLACK HILLS

THE Black Hills are an outlying group of the Rockies, so far removed from the main series of ridges as to be almost unrelated. Roundabout them for hundreds of miles the country is a monotony of low hills and plains which offers a striking contrast to this medley of craggy uplifts and irregular valleys. Harney Peak, the monarch of the Black Hills group reaches an elevation of over seven thousand feet, but the immediate vicinity is itself so high that neither Harney nor any of the other mountains are especially impressive. On the slopes and heights grow dark forests of pine, and in the vales is pasturage and many a sunny well-watered glade where are occasional small cultivated fields and rude farmhouses.

One advantage the Black Hills inhabitants claim to have over the dwellers on the plains is that their region is immune from tornadoes. "Since I've been here," said one old resident, "we've never had enough of a gale to take the shingles off a woodshed."

But I was informed that in some of the outlying foothill hamlets the wind at times blew so that the people "could hardly keep the buttons on their clothes."

Considerable mellow soil has gathered in the valley pockets, yet rocks are for the most part omnipresent, often thrusting up great ragged ridges to a height of hundreds of feet. Mica is plentiful in the rocks, and the soil is full of glittering particles that have a very pretty sheen and sparkle in the sunshine. Then, too, you see many scattered fragments of quartz as clear as crystal, and though the quartz and the pulverized mica have no value they attract and please the eye, and are suggestive of hidden wealth.

The discovery of gold in the Black Hills is usually attributed to a government exploring expedition which spent the summer of 1874 in the region; but even at that time there were a good many miners roaming around prospecting, entirely independent of the troops. The miners found gold, and so did the soldiers, and both told stories of wealth to be found in the Hills that created great interest throughout the country and at once gave the group of wild mountains world-wide fame.

For a number of years the floating population of the frontier had been suffering from a dearth of exciting mineral discoveries, and they promptly made ready to rush in. Numerous other fortune-seekers were attracted from the older Eastern states. The fact that they would be trespassers on the choicest hunting-ground belonging to the Sioux Indians was no serious deterrent. Men have always been ready to risk their lives for gold; and the rights of Indians do not usually count for much with the whites. The government, however, had included the Black Hills in the Sioux reservation, and, to avoid trouble, the authorities at Washington endeavored to keep the miners out. They soon realized the hopelessness of the attempt, if the Hills were rich in gold, and started negotiations to buy the tract from its owners. This they succeeded in doing in 1876, but fortune-seekers were numerous in the Hills long before the transfer was made.

"People went crazy about gold," one old-timer said to me; "and though the soldiers took a good many men out of the reservation the population was increasing right along. Men who were used to mining and to rough frontier life couldn't have been driven away with a club. They were bound to keep on gold-hunting in spite of everything. I know an old man who's a fair sample of what those fellows were then. All the soldiers in the United States couldn't keep him away from a mining camp. In his day he made quite a lot of money; but it has all slipped away from him. Still he sticks to mining, and he's out in the mountains prospecting now. He hunts around and picks up stones that look promising, pounds 'em up in a mortar and pans out the stuff to see if there's gold in it. He's all alone, and some day he'll be found dead in his little shack.

"My pardner and me come here in the spring of '75. The soldiers didn't ketch us, and we was in the town of Custer when the big strike of gold was made early the next year in Deadwood. It was toward the end of winter, and there was still snow on the ground, but everybody who could leave started off for the new diggings. We'd thought Custer was going to be the big town of the Black Hills; and yet almost in a night it was depopulated. There were fourteen hundred buildings in the place, and only fourteen persons remained in town; so there were a hundred buildings to each person.

"It's funny how people will hustle off that way. They are just like a lot of cattle stampeded in a storm—each going with the crowd in a mad rush and not seeing or thinking. A feller will tell about a prospect that he thinks is going to be a money-maker. The next man who tells the story enlarges on it a little, and by the time it's passed through half a dozen hands everybody goes wild. Off they start for the new camp; but even if no one makes a cent there's not a man among 'em who isn't happy until he's broke.

"I didn't make any lucky gold strikes myself and presently I tried work of another sort. In the spring of '77 I carted hay forty or fifty miles from the borders of the Hills to Deadwood. I had eight oxen and carried about two tons to a load. The hay cost me thirty dollars a ton, and I sold it for fourteen cents a pound. Supplies of all sorts were scarce here in those days, and the stock in Deadwood really suffered for food. I wasn't long in disposing of what I brought. I'd stop in the middle of the street, and men would crowd around the load like a swarm of bees, and hold up their money to buy. The hay was tied up with light rope into bundles that sold for a hundred pounds- but which didn't weigh much over seventy-five. As soon as my cart was emptied I'd turn around and come back to where there was prairie and a chance for the oxen to graze. I couldn't have afforded to feed them in Deadwood.

"I was out and around alone a good deal; and yet with all the travelling I did I never saw any Indians. I didn't want to see any. They weren't friendly toward the whites, and I was always more or less anxious about 'em. So were the other people who came into the region. But I was more afraid of lawless white men. They'd dress up in imitation of the savages—paint themselves and put on blankets and fasten a horsetail on the back of their heads to look like long Indian hair. Then they'd rob the stage and the poor tenderfoot who was coming in with money. Lots of misdeeds were laid to the Indians where they weren't to blame at all. What the outlaws liked best was to hold up the coaches when they heard that bullion was going to be shipped out; but now and then the owners of the bullion would fool the robbers by filling the bags with sand.

"The nearest I came to running afoul of Indians was one morning on my way to Deadwood with a load of hay. I came to a spot where a party of whites had camped the night before, and found a woman dead beside the road. It was a pretty bad place for Indians—handy for game and water, and just the spot they'd naturally pick out for a camp. They had turned loose on the whites at about daylight, and of co'se the whites skipped out. They didn't know what they was doing—this outfit didn't. All but one woman escaped up a hill. The horses was so scared they stampeded, and the Indians couldn't get them; and there was no chance to steal from the wagons because the whites were all the time shooting. In a little while the Indians left. Pretty soon afterward I happened along, and there lay the dead woman, and the rest of the company was hollering on the bluff.

"No one was safe from the Indians in the first year or two. They would crawl up the high hills and shoot at the men working in the gulches below, and the miners used to keep their guns handy, and they provided defences for emergencies.

"The last Indian rising was in 1892. One of the old heads went into a trance. He said the Messiah appeared to him and ordered the Indians to drive out the whites, and promised that the deer and buffalo would return so the Indians would have their happy hunting-ground to themselves again. They began to massacre the whites; but the troops soon put a stop to that sort of thing. The savages might have made more of a fight if they hadn't been so afraid of cannon. Let 'em hear the discharge of a cannon, and they think the world is coming to an end. With just one cannon you can scare a whole tribe. Often you don't even need to fire it; to show it on a knoll is sufficient."

The man whose comments I have reported was a citizen of Custer where I spent some time rambling about the region. The town has never recovered from the famous exodus that depopulated it in its youth, and is merely a village in a glade of the rocky uplands. As a matter of fact the only really notable mine in the Black Hills is the "Homestake" near Deadwood. This employs nearly two thousand men under ground and is one of the richest gold mines in America. The first prospectors looked around the neighborhood late in 1874, and other parties came drifting in the next year; but there was no special excitement till a twelve-month later. Deadwood Gulch, where gold was first found in quantity, was then covered with a dense growth of pine, much of it dead and mingled with a nearly impassable tangle of underbrush.

The biggest strike was made by a man named Wheeler. He is said to have cleaned up over one hundred thousand dollars, and then to have asked and obtained an escort of soldiers to see him safely across the wilderness to the nearest railway station, two hundred miles distant. What became of him and his fortune afterward no one could tell me. If he went away satisfied with the wealth he had accumulated he was a very exceptional miner. Usually the lucky ones embarked on new ventures and lost their earlier gains. The chances were always fascinating, but where one made money, thousands of other adventurers made nothing at all. Perhaps the commonest source of profit to those who discovered "a prospect" was to sell it to moneyed Eastern men. The purchasers, as a rule, not only put their money in the ground but left it there.

During the spring and summer of 1876, each day, and almost each hour, witnessed the arrival of new parties of gold seekers in Deadwood Gulch. Whoever could saw a board or drive a nail commanded his own price, and in a short time the place grew from a few log cabins to a city of seven thousand inhabitants. The hotels were so crowded it was considered a luxury to occupy a chair in the office during the night. Everything was extremely expensive. Bread went as high as a dollar a loaf, and people were glad to get it at that price. One man with whom I talked declared that the high cost of living was a result of modern trust methods among the merchants.

"They were pretty smart," said he, "and were careful not to let too many supplies come in at a time to lower the price. If they had a load of flour on the way they'd drive out with a buggy and meet it and have it stop or come slower. They'd carry back just a few sacks and say the team was delayed by bad roads.

"But no one minded those little tricks then. Everybody come in with plenty of money, and they expected to be able to get plenty more when that was gone. A good many of the gold-seekers was fetched in by Joe Vollin, who had a freighting outfit going back and forth between the Black Hills and the Missouri. He charged 'em twenty-five dollars a head, and they had to walk all the way. But they were allowed to put their little baggage—a couple of blankets and a satchel—on the wagon. If the wagon got stuck in the mud, a rope would be hitched to the end of the tongue, and the tenderfeet would get hold and help pull the thing out on firmer ground. You take seventy-five or a hundred men and they can pull a dickins of a load. They worked their way and paid their fare, too; but they thought that was all right. They'd never been in a wild country before, so it was easy for Vollin to scare 'em with his Indian stories, and they had no hankering to go ahead by themselves.

"Often they didn't know what to do when they got here. They'd thought the gold would be lying around right on the surface of the ground. It was their idea they could walk along the cricks and pick up the gold in lumps. When they found they'd have to work for it, and that there was nothing to be seen but dirt and rocks and wild woodland many a feller got sick of the proposition about the second day and was ready to pay Vollin another twenty-five dollars to be allowed to walk back to civilization alongside of one of the freighting wagons."

The placer mines of Deadwood Gulch and the tributary ravines were for a short time very remunerative, and the town that grew up there was the metropolis of the Black Hills. Thither the miners from all the region around wended their way every Saturday night with their weekly accumulation of gold dust and nuggets. Gold in these forms was the commonest kind of currency in the Hills, and everyone carried a bottle or sack of it for use in place of money. On arriving in Deadwood at the week-end the average miner proceeded to spend his golden wealth like a nabob; and on Monday morning, with a fresh supply of "grub" thrown over his shoulder he returned to his claim to delve for more of the precious metal. No doubt he was cheered at his rough labor by the certainty of having another "good time" the next Sunday. That was the busiest and noisiest day of the week in Deadwood. The streets were crowded both with buckskin-clothed mountaineers, and with recent arrivals from the East. You heard the blows of hammers and the rasping of saws where buildings were being erected. Here a gambler was crying his game, and there a street preacher was exhorting sinners to repent.

As to preachers, one finds very little veneration for them among the mining folk—at least in fair weather. "We never was much for going to church," remarked a pioneer of the region. "You can't make no money that way, and a miner has something else to do besides attending to religion. It's curious, but it's a fact, that when a preacher wanted to build a church or anything of that sort he was sure to get most of the money off the gamblers and liquor sellers. Naturally they can't collect much from their religious church members, because a man that prays all the time can't be expected to earn or have much money. Such men perhaps give ten cents or a quarter apiece, while from each saloon the minister will get ten or twenty dollars. Then he'll give the liquor sellers thunder in church the next Sunday. Religion is only society—I call it. You take away the social attraction, and you'd have nothing left. In fact, there are not many people in the world who believe very seriously in religion unless they're weak in the mind. Still, it's good enough for young people and puts a kind of fear in 'em they never forget. But you can't put much fear into an old man like me. I'm glad though to have my children attend church. It keeps 'em down a little. They'll learn fast enough."

The only local clergyman who seems to have gained a permanent place in the hearts of the mining folk is one who was killed by the Indians while on his way to a neighboring village where he was to preach. He knew the danger, and yet duty called and he took the risk. This heroism and the tragic result brought him what no amount of exhortation would have gained, and he is one of the Black Hills saints. High on the terrace of a bluff above the town is the cemetery overlooking the narrow glen, and there the martyr preacher is honored with a full-length brown-stone statue which has an inclosing coop of chicken-wire fencing to protect it from the affection of those who would like to chip off mementoes.

A still more popular hero, similarly memorialized, was "Wild Bill." While on a visit to the region to see what the country was like he was shot dead as he was playing in one of the gambling places. So far as I could learn he was of the ordinary type of frontiersman—not a desperado as his name and manner of death might suggest—but with the usual frontier virtues and failings. He had been a scout in the Civil War and had served in a like capacity on the plains. There was no fear in his make-up, but he well knew that he had enemies, and he took the precaution, whenever he sat down indoors, to place himself with his back to the wall. But this did not save him from a violent end.

A marble bust on a pedestal formerly marked his grave in the cemetery, but the relic hunters did some busting on their own account after the sculptor finished, and soon the monument was ruined. Then fresh contributions were levied, and now the visitor to the cemetery sees a full-length brown-stone figure of a bare-headed, long-haired plainsman, standing in a wire coop like that which protects the martyr preacher. In one hand the effigy holds a pistol and is about to draw another from his cartridge belt. It is a rather belligerent looking figure for that silent city of the dead, and its grotesqueness has been made the more emphatic by painting the pupils of the eyes blue.

Another contemporary notable was "Calamity Jane." This name appears to have been her chief stock in trade, and about the only reason for her being remembered. She was shiftless and vicious—an idling dare-devil who was in her glory when she dressed up partly in man's clothes and partly in woman's and walked around the the streets to be greeted as "Calamity Jane." No monument marks her resting-place—possibly because there was nothing startling about the manner of her death.

In the turmoil of the first year or two of the gold excitement Deadwood was a rough town. It was full of gamblers, and shooting was a common pastime. But this period soon passed, and the place became as orderly and well-governed as most of its sort. That does not mean it was ideal; for drinkers, gamblers, and other purveyors or indulgers in dissipation are allowed to do much more as they please in mining towns than in the average community.

By reason of its situation the town is particularly piquant and interesting, and it has a pleasing air of stability and comfort. The homes cling along the declivities of the deep gulch, and creep far up every side ravine. Some of the streets with their attendant board sidewalks are marvels of steepness; and the houses are arranged in terraces, each row looking down on the roofs of those below. In the depths of the hollow are the railroads and a swift muddy creek, business blocks, mines, shops and other buildings, all jumbled together and entirely lacking elbow-room. Roundabout rise the lofty wooded ridges with here and there a perpendicular crag, or a hilltop crowned with monumental ledges and heaps of boulders. It seems a fitting place for Nature to have exercised her magic in making the gold which has directly or indirectly been the means of drawing most of the population to this rugged region.

NOTE.—The Black Hills cover a stretch of country about one hundred miles in length by fifty in width. They rise abruptly from the surface of a level prairie country and reach altitudes varying from three thousand to seven thousand feet. It is evident that with their streams and crags and pine-clad slopes they must contain not a little scenery that is ruggedly attractive. There are many picturesque villages in the valleys, and a leisurely traveller who likes rambling on foot or riding on horseback finds much to enjoy. The town that is most strikingly interesting in its setting, and in its romantic history, is Deadwood. Several other places that have considerable attraction, either commercial or scenic, are near at hand, and among these is the city of Lead, where is located the great Homestake Mine.

BASIC FACTS

Capital City .... Pierre
Nickname .... The Coyote State
Flower .... Pasque Flower
Bird .... Ringnecked Pheasant
Tree .... Black Hills Spruce
Song .... *Hail, South Dakota*
Stone .... Black Hills Gold
Animal .... Coyote
Entered the Union .... November 2, 1889

STATISTICS*

Land Area (square miles) 75,955
    Rank in Nation 16th
Population† 680,000
    Rank in Nation 44th
    Density per square mile 9.0
Number of Representatives in Congress 2
Capital City .... Pierre
    Population 9,699
    Rank in State 9th
Largest City .... Sioux Falls
    Population 72,488
Number of Cities over 10,000 Population 8
Number of Counties 67

---

* Based on 1970 census statistics compiled by the Bureau of the Census.
† Estimated by Bureau of the Census for July 1, 1972.

MAP OF CONGRESSIONAL DISTRICTS
OF SOUTH DAKOTA

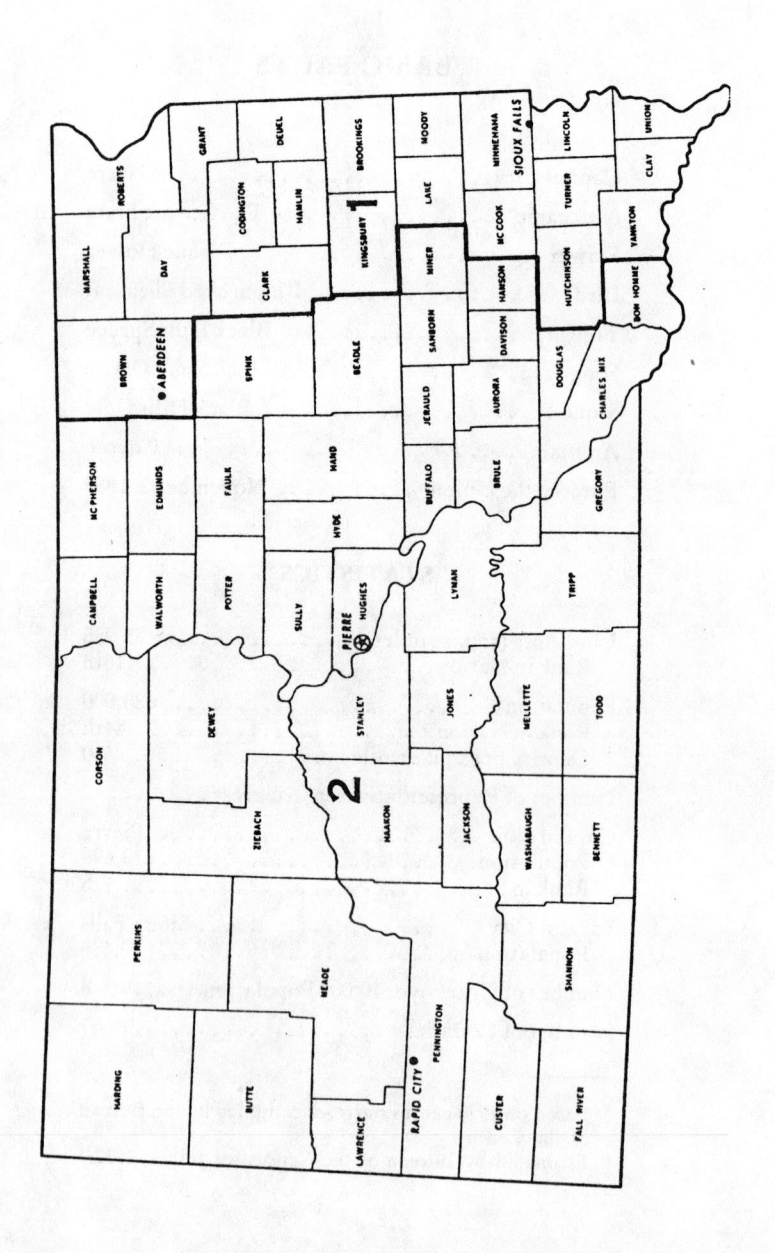

SELECTED BIBLIOGRAPHY

Coursey, Oscar William. *Literature of South Dakota*.
    Mitchell, S. D.: The Educator Supply Company,
    1925.

Putney, Effie Florence. *In the South Dakota Country*.
    Mitchel, S. D.: Educator Supply Company, 1922.

Robinson, Doane. *History of South Dakota*. Logansport,
    Ind.: B. F. Bowen and Company, 1904. 2 vols.

_____. *South Dakota*. Chicago and New York:
    The American Historical Society, Inc., 1930.

Schell, Herbert Samuel. *History of South Dakota*.
    Lincoln: University of Nebraska Press, 1961.

_____. *South Dakota, Its Beginnings
    and Growth*. New York: American Book Company, 1960.

Smith, G. M. *History and Government of South Dakota*.
    New York and Cincinnati: American Book Company,
    1912.

NAME INDEX

Adams, John Quincy, 3
Anderson, Sigurd, 14
Armstrong, Moses Kendall, 4
Atkinson, Henry, 1
Audobon, John J., 2

Beadle, William Henry Harrison, 7
Bennett, Granville G., 11
Bennett, John E., 11
Berry, Thomas, 13
Boe, Nils A., 15
Borglum, Gutzon, 13
Brookings, Wilmot W., 3
Brown, Alfred, 7
Bryan, William Jennings, 10
Bulow, William J., 13
Bushfield, Harlan J., 13
Byrne, Frank M., 12

Campbell, Norman B., 4
Carson, Dighton, 11
Carter, Jimmy, 17
Clark, Newton, 4
Clark, William, 1
Clay, Henry, 3
Codington, G. S. S., 7
Crawford, Coe I., 11
Custer, George Armstrong, 6

Davison, Henry C., 4
Day, Merritt H., 7
Devel, Jacob S., 3
Dewey, William Pitt, 5
Dole, Robert J., 17
Douglas, Stephen A., 5

Edmunds, Newton, 5
Elrod, Samuel H., 11

Fenner, Frank, 15
Fischer, Mrs. Andrew, 15

Ford, Gerald R., 17
Foss, Joe J., 14
Frémont, John C., 2

Green, Warren E., 13
Gubbard, Archie, 15
Gunderson, Carl, 13

Haakon VII, King of Norway, 12
Hanson, Joseph R., 4
Harding, J. A., 11
Harris, Edward, 2
Harrison, Benjamin, 9
Heart, George, 7
Herreid, Charles N., 10
Herseth, Ralph E., 14
Hickock, Wild Bill, 7
Hutchinson, John, 4

Jackson, John R., 12
Jensen, Leslie, 13
Jerauld, H. A., 8
Joseph, Louis, 9

Kneip, Richard F., 16, 17

Lee, Andrew F., 10
Levi, Edward H., 17
Lewis, Meriwether, 1
Lincoln, Abraham, 3
Lisa, Manuel, 1
Lyman, W. P., 5

Marshall, William Rainey, 2
Maximilian of Neuweid, Prince, 2
McCook, Edwin S., 5
McGovern, George, 16
McMaster, William H., 12
McPherson, James Birdseye, 5
Meade, George Gordon, 9
Means, Russell, 16, 17
Mellette, Arthur C., 9, 11
Mickelson, George T., 14
Miner, Ephraim, 5
Miner, Nelson, 5
Mix, Charles E., 3

Mondale, Walter F., 17
Moody, Gideon Curtis, 5
Mundt, Karl, 16

Norbeck, Peter, 12

O'Fallon, Benjamin, 1

Pennington, John L., 6
Perkins, Henry E., 11
Potter, Joel A., 7

Reifel, Ben, 15
Roberts, S. G., 8

Sanborn, George W., 8
Shannon, Peter C., 6
Sharpe, Merrell Q., 14

Sheldon, Charles H., 10
Sitting Bull, Sioux Indian Chief, 10
Spink, Solomon Lewis, 5
Stanley, David Sloane, 5
Sully, Alfred, 6

Thomas, John, 17
Towne, Charles A., 10
Tripp, Bartlett, 6
Turner, John W., 4

Vérendrye, Francois de la, 1
Vessey, Robert S., 11

Washabaugh, Frank J., 8
Wilson, Richard, 16

Ziebach, Frank M., 12

R01 0846 7832